D0857378

CONTAGIOUS
EMOTIONS

CONTAGIOUS EMOTIONS

▼

*Staying Well
When Your Loved One
Is Depressed*

▲

RONALD M. PODELL, M.D.,

with PORTER SHIMER

POCKET BOOKS

New York   London   Toronto   Sydney   Tokyo   Singapore

For
Alyson, Josh, and Alex

POCKET BOOKS, a division of Simon & Schuster Inc.
1230 Avenue of the Americas, New York, NY 10020

Copyright © 1992 by Ronald M. Podell, M.D.

All rights reserved, including the right to reproduce
this book or portions thereof in any form whatsoever.
For information address Pocket Books,
a division of Simon & Schuster Inc.,
1230 Avenue of the Americas, New York, NY 10020

Podell, Ronald M.
   Contagious emotions : staying well when your loved one is
depressed / Ronald M. Podell, with Porter Shimer.
      p. cm.
   Includes bibliographical references.
   ISBN: 0-671-70239-4 : $20.00
   1. Depression, Mental—Case studies.   2. Depressed persons—Family
relationships—Case studies.   3. Family psychotherapy—Case studies.
I. Shimer, Porter.   II. Title.
RC537.P62   1992
616.85′27—dc20   91-31725
                                                                                          CIP

First Pocket Books hardcover printing May 1992

10 9 8 7 6 5 4 3 2 1

POCKET and colophon are registered trademarks of
Simon & Schuster Inc.

Printed in the U.S.A.

ACKNOWLEDGMENTS

There are many people to thank. Since this is my first book, I want to thank those who have contributed directly to it as well as those who have contributed to my life so that there could be a book.

Mel Kinder was the pathfinder for this book and very much a mentor for the proposal that sold it. It was Mel who read my final proposal and said, "You're talking about emotional contagion." I hope Westridge has helped shrink your "misery gap," Mel.

Next there is Suzanne Wickham, who saw the need for the book and showed insight far above her superiors.

I would like to thank Leslie Wells, my editor, for believing in the project and for nursing it through both calm and troubled waters. Richard Pine, my agent, was both a super salesman and a steady guide for a new author. He has my sincere gratitude for his help and support.

Porter Shimer's melodic writing speaks for itself, but my thanks to Porter goes for his willingness to share his own pain and inner self. His courage helped make the book more alive and genuine.

Hank Weisinger not only helped structure the proposal, but I can honestly say that there would be no book without him. I do not believe I would have ever tried to write a book without his encouragement, support, caring, and friendship.

I want to thank Rocky Gerner for reviewing the professional-help chapter and for teaching me to enjoy the art of psychopharmacology as well as the art of psychotherapy.

There are people I want to honor who have made my life emotionally rich, and any success I have must be largely connected to their loving relationships with me. I want to thank my parents, Sid and Pearl Podell, for their love and genuine support of my vision of my own life. I learned as much about therapy from working with my father in his pharmacy as I did in my psychiatry residency. My sister Lynn has always been a dear and special person who has given me great inner motivation and support. Dr. Herb Poch, my uncle, was the model after whom I fashioned my career. Both he and my Aunt Leila were always in my corner from the minute I was born.

I have been fortunate to have a loving, caring family and good friends to support me. I tried to honor you by using your names for the case histories as a way of telling you that I care, and that you're special to Alyson, Josh, Alex, and me.

My dedication of the book to my wife and two children speaks to the support, understanding, and love that they have brought to my life. They tolerated the long hours I spent in front of the computer better than I did, and Alyson patiently listened to my obsessions with undying support and encouragement.

Finally, I want to thank my patients, who helped me learn what is in this book, and with whom I have shared very special relationships that have made my life more meaningful and rewarding.

CONTENTS

PART THREE

▼

COMING OUT A WINNER

PART ONE

What You're Up Against

VICTIMS OF AN INVISIBLE FORCE:
The Power of Fusion

"If you live with a lame man, you will learn to limp."

PLUTARCH, A.D. 96–120

Dear Dr. Podell,

I'm writing to you because I attended your lecture on mood disorders at the university, and I was hoping you might be able to help. I think I'm living with the kind of person you were talking about, and I don't know how much longer I can take it. My husband can be in a good mood one minute, but then blow up over almost nothing and become miserable and mean. And if I try to comfort him, he gets even worse.

He accuses me of being responsible for his bad moods and says that if I'd just leave him alone, he'd be fine. But I don't think he would be. I think there are things bothering him that *he doesn't want to talk about. Why else would he be drinking so much, and not sleeping? I've been trying to get him to see a counselor, but he says he doesn't need to. He almost seems to like being the way he is, but I can't understand how. He doesn't have any close friends, he never has any fun with the children, and he doesn't get any pleasure from being with me anymore. We haven't slept together in three months.*

I'm worried and confused. Could my husband be right when he says I'm the one to blame? He says I'm like the pot calling the kettle black, that I'm the one who needs the help. And, in away, I guess he's right. I'm short-tempered with the children, and I've been drinking in the afternoons to help me relax before he gets home from work. I'm embarrassed to tell you that sometimes I hate him.

It just seems that so much is going wrong now, and nothing I do seems to make it any better. My husband got into a shoving match with our 16-year-old son the other night, and our 9-year-old daughter became hysterical. Our home just isn't a happy place anymore, and it makes me very sad. I never thought this could happen to us, because there used to be so much love.

I'm starting to cry so I'm going to stop now. Please call me if you can help.

Thank you,
Sharon

I received that letter from Sharon seven years ago, but I can still remember where I was and what I did. I was having lunch at a small café across the street from our newly founded Center for Mood Disorders, and I later went back to the office and had my secretary arrange for an appointment with Sharon as soon as possible.

Her situation wasn't that extreme or even unique, but that was precisely what I found so upsetting. It was so common. I was seeing it over and over in my practice when I would ask to meet with the family members of the depressed patients I was treating. Almost without fail, they were suffering just as Sharon was.

They were confused, frustrated, worried, scared, angry, and depressed. They were feeling many of the same emotions, in fact, as their disturbed loved ones who were under my care. It was as though they had "caught" these emotions from their depressed loved ones, just as if they had been exposed to a contagious physical disease.

I began investigating this contagious aspect of depression more closely in my own patients and in other case histories in the psychiatric literature. Depression *was* a contagious disorder, I decided. It could spread just like any cold or flu, infecting all who came in close contact with it. Not only could the spouses of depressed people become distraught, but the children, parents, and even friends and coworkers of depressed people could experience negative effects.

Yet, had I been warned of this "contagiousness" in all my years of medical and psychiatric training?

Amazingly, I had not. Nor had most of my colleagues. This was new therapeutic territory, something that had been grossly overlooked in the clinical practice of psychiatry, and yet it was something vital to both the understanding and the treatment of the epidemic of depression we have in this country today. By infecting those around them, depressed people inadvertently create the very environment their depression needs to thrive.

As an example, Sharon's husband was unintentionally galvanizing his own disturbed state by causing emotional disturbances in his wife and children. The disturbed environment he was creating was allowing him to deny that he had an emotional problem. He could tell himself that he was merely reacting as anyone would to a depressing atmosphere—an atmosphere *he* was helping to create. This is one of the most problematic aspects of many types of depressive disorders. They literally blind their sufferers to both the consequences and the reasons for their actions.

When I explained this to Sharon during our first session,

she seemed relieved at first. "I was really beginning to think it was me," she said. "He can get me so upset that I really start to think I'm going crazy."

"But in a way you are going a little crazy," I had to tell her. "Yes, it's your husband who's provoking you, but if you'll stop to think about some of the things you've done at the peaks of your anger, and some of the thoughts you've had in the depths of your despair, I think you'll have to agree they weren't normal, and they certainly weren't helpful."

"But isn't it natural to express yourself when you feel you've been hurt or wronged?" she asked.

Of course it is, I told her, and that's just the problem. When you live with a depressed person, you get into trouble precisely because you *do* react naturally. You allow your gut reactions to pull you closer to the very "germs" that wind up giving you your loved one's "disease." This is precisely the aspect that makes depression such a contagious force.

Depression Is the Fuel, But Fusion Is the Fire

Sharon's case was a very important one for me because in many ways it helped me pull together some missing pieces. Not all relationships, I decided, were equally vulnerable to the contagious-emotions phenomenon. If a couple or two family members had a very stable and loving relationship before depression set in, relatively little damage would occur.

But if problems existed prior to the onset of a mood disturbance, the anxiety and depression would pry the relationship apart at all of its weakest points. The longer this prying apart went on, moreover, the harder it was to pull the relationship back together. In the most extreme cases, fatal damage could be done that would make a relationship burst apart and dissolve forever.

Sharon turned out to be lucky in two respects. Not only did she and her husband have a basically sound and caring relationship before his depression occurred, but she had come to me in time. My sessions with Sharon went extremely well. She was able to understand the role she inadvertently had been playing in her husband's illness, we were able to convince him to undergo appropriate treatment, and the two were able to grow even stronger from their experience.

Such smooth sailing is not always the case, however, when a relationship falls prey to depression. In many relationships, a destructive, invisible force begins to develop that distorts every aspect of relating, but particularly communication. I saw couples being victimized by this contagious, invisible force time and time again as I talked to them in my office.

We'd begin our discussions in a dignified manner, but just one spark of controversy would ignite a chain reaction of intensely aggressive and malicious exchanges. Ghosts suddenly came out of the closet in herds, blows were aimed below the belt, and suddenly I was looking at an emotional holocaust. The anger had escalated at a rate that seemed downright nuclear.

Suddenly it hit me: I *was* looking at something "nuclear." I was looking at a chain reaction not of atomic particles but of human emotions—emotions that once in motion were unstoppable until they had run their destructive course. I decided to call this force "fusion."

We'll be looking at fusion in greater detail as this book unfolds, but let me say for now that fused relationships are characterized by *reactivity* and *contagious emotions*. If your partner is angry, anxious, or depressed, you find yourself feeling the same way. Each of you becomes convinced that what you feel, say, and do is a *logical reaction* to what your loved one is saying and doing. Similarly, conversations and arguments in fused relationships become circular—each of you blames the other for causing problems and provoking bad feelings—and boundaries become so unclear that it is confusing as to whose thoughts and feelings are whose, and which one has "problems" and which doesn't. Fusion is a highly injurious but all-too-common element in relationship conflicts where mood disturbances play a role. Depression may be the fuel, but fusion is the fire.

I started observing my depressed patients and their loved ones with this fusion force in mind, and its validity became progressively clearer to me as I did. Fusion made these couples behave in ways that were virtually beyond their control. They said things they didn't really mean, and hurt each other in ways that later would cause them deep regret. They simply could not control themselves when caught in fusion's grip. They behaved as though they were bitter enemies fighting for their very lives.

MARRIAGE/MAYHEM: THE CASE OF TOM AND MARSHA

Several years had passed since my meetings with Sharon, and I was learning to observe and understand the contagious-emotions phenomenon—and fusion—more with each couple I'd see. If I was treating a depressed patient, I began to make it a practice to always ask to see the spouse or close family members. I found that, inevitably, they would also be in need of my help. But many times it would happen the other way around— I'd first be visited by the spouse, from whom I would learn that his or her depressed partner was the one most in need of my treatment. I present to you now the case of Marsha and Tom, which illustrates this quite well.

"I just seem to be losing my energy for life," Marsha, an attractive, well-dressed person, said to me as she sat sullenly in my office the first time we met. "Here I am, 46 years old; a time when life should be getting easier, but it seems to be getting harder. I used to keep so busy and be so cheerful, but lately I've been having trouble even getting out of bed."

I told Marsha just to relax and tell me whatever she thought I should know. I could tell from her expressions and tone of voice that she had been in emotional pain for quite some time.

"I'm not sure where to begin," she said.

"Are you married?" I asked.

"I guess you could call it that," she answered.

And with that, we were off and running. Marsha went on to tell me of a marriage that had been heading slowly downhill for the past five to ten of its twenty-two years. Her husband, Tom, had always been moody, but in the past several years—and especially in the past few months—he had been getting noticeably worse.

"It's gotten so that I don't know who's going to be coming home at night for dinner," she said. "Is it going to be the happy Tom, the sad Tom, or the mean Tom? He can be all three, but I never know which one will show up. I try to cheer him up when he's sad, but that doesn't work, and I try to calm him down when he's angry, but that doesn't work, either. Nothing I do seems to make any difference. If anything, I only make his moods worse."

The more I quizzed Marsha about her husband, the more I suspected that his behavior was a major factor in how she had been feeling. She went on to talk of disciplinary problems she had been having with their three children, of her failure in her career in real estate sales, and of trouble she'd been having sleeping, but always she would include something that had been said or done by Tom.

"When he's in a good mood, I feel great, almost like I've won the lottery. But when he's in his other moods, it's getting to be more than I can handle. When he's sad, he has the hurt-little-boy look on his face that makes me want to cry. He'll just sit in front of the television when he's like that and not say a word for hours. But then when he's in one of his mean moods, he can be terrifying. He'll usually go right for the liquor cabinet when he comes home like that and pour himself a large vodka. And that's when the insults begin. He'll start picking on me about anything he can think of, but usually about how I'm interested in him only for his money, and how I couldn't survive on my own if my life depended on it. It hurts, because in some ways it's true, but I worked hard when I was in real estate, and I've tried hard to be a good wife and a good mother. It upsets me that he doesn't seem to understand what I'm going through."

Marsha was becoming tearful at this point and our hour was nearly up, so I suggested we stop. I asked her to be prepared to tell me more about her husband in our next session, however, because I suspected Tom's emotional disturbance might be more serious—and more relevant to her own state of mind—than she realized. She agreed and we scheduled another appointment for the following week.

"I just don't think I can take it anymore," were her first words as we started that next session. "Friday night he came home late in one of his worst moods ever, and on Saturday he stayed in bed until three in the afternoon. Then he had a big blowup with our 14-year-old daughter Saturday evening over dinner and disappeared into the bedroom for the rest of the night. I'm really getting worried, Doctor, because he made the remark in his fight with our daughter that none of us really care about him, and that maybe we'd all be better off if he were dead. I'm scared."

I was concerned, too, because Tom's case sounded like others I'd seen before—chronic depression in an aggressive male manifesting itself as anger, despair, denial, and substance abuse as the depressed person seeks to blame his depressed moods on the uncaring attitudes of others. The result becomes the very fusion that Marsha and her children were experiencing—hellish skirmishes that cause feelings of anger, despair, and blame to escalate even higher. There was no question in my mind at this point that Tom's depression—and the fusion it was causing—was the primary reason for Marsha's disturbed state. She was allowing her sense of self-worth to spiral down right along with her husband's—a vicious cycle in that the worse Tom felt, the more upset Marsha became; and the more upset Marsha became, the worse Tom felt. It was fusion at its classic worst.

Tom's behavior of the past few weeks, however, indicated to me that his ongoing chronic depression was slipping into a more serious major depression in which suicide was a very real possibility. Intervention clearly would be necessary if Tom's illness—and the toxic environment it was creating for Marsha and the children—was going to stand a chance of being cured.

"Would it be possible to include Tom in our next session?" I asked Marsha.

She doubted if she could get him to come, but she said she'd do what she could. I suggested she tell Tom that I felt his input would be valuable in helping me to treat her. This suggestion evidently worked, as Tom was there by Marsha's side in my waiting room one week later.

Tom was a large man, tanned, well dressed, and very fit. Yet I could tell right away that he was troubled. His brow was furrowed, he appeared morose, and he seemed to have difficulty concentrating on my questions. When I asked him why he thought Marsha had come to see me, he said it was because she was feeling depressed about her failing real estate career, and because she was having disciplinary problems with the children. When I asked how he had been feeling, he stared at Marsha for a moment before answering.

"I've been feeling a little down lately, but I'll get over it," he said.

"Marsha tells me you've been a little unpredictablé lately, feeling good on occasion, but pretty lousy at other times. Do you know why that might be?"

I could see an immediate shift in Tom's demeanor—from sullen to defensive.

"She's a worrier," he said. "It gives her something to do."

Marsha shifted her gaze dejectedly to the floor.

"What's she worried about?" I asked.

"Everything. Me. The children. Her career. Her health. My health. You name it, and she can worry about it."

"I'm worried about you because I love you," Marsha interjected.

"No, you're worried about me because you're worried about yourself. I'm your meal ticket—that's the bottom line," Tom exploded.

I could see we were on the brink of a fusion eruption, which I knew would destroy all chances for further discussion in a rational manner. I stepped in to calm things down.

"Marsha came to see me because she's been depressed herself. She feels that your relationship is falling apart," I said. "She's concerned about how you've been feeling, and she thinks you've grown more and more depressed over the past month. My professional opinion is that you need psychiatric treatment. I think you're suffering from chronic depression that's been with you for several years, but which has progressed into a more serious major depression during the last month. Depression is an illness and needs to be treated both medically and psychologically, and I believe I can help you. I also believe that your wife has been seriously affected by your depression and is going to require some treatment herself so that she can also recover and stop inadvertently making your condition worse."

I was concerned that I might get more denial and animosity from Tom after this confrontation, but I got just the opposite. Tears formed in his eyes as he suddenly began talking about a phone call he had received several months before, shortly before his father's death.

"He was calling to make up. After fifteen years, he was calling to make up, and I hung up on him. How was I to know he was so sick? Three weeks later, he was dead."

Marsha reached over to console Tom following his revelation, but he pulled away and stood up to gaze out the window. I quietly suggested to Marsha that she return to the waiting room to let Tom and me finish the session alone.

In Marsha's absence, Tom revealed that he had never told her much about his relationship with his father, but that it had upset him very much. He had cut ties with his father following a falling out over a joint business venture over ten years before, but the two had always had a stormy relationship. His father would never give him the support or praise that Tom needed. "I could never tell if he really didn't think much of me, or if he was jealous of me. But all we did was fight, so I finally just cut the ties altogether."

It became clear in the remainder of our discussion that Tom's recent major depression had been triggered in large part by his father's death. Tom's conflicted feelings of anger, guilt, and love were proving to be just too much for him to bear. He had always prided himself on being emotionally indestructible, but this—on top of the troubles he'd been having with Marsha— was exceeding his abilities to cope.

Tom agreed to begin treatment with me following that session, and we progressed quite well. We discovered that Tom unconsciously had been punishing his wife for the anger and frustration he had been feeling in his relationship with his father. And when his father died, those feelings escalated because they became fueled with intense guilt. Tom was angry at himself, in addition to still being angry at his father. Poor Marsha took the heat. All this was the background for the distorted, negative thoughts that Tom carried with him about his expectations of being perfect and successful and his unyielding desire for approval from the authority figures in his life. Tom was a setup for depression, based on his distorted, negative thoughts, his genetic inheritance, and his early childhood experiences.

I won't go into the details of what it took to resolve Tom and Marsha's differences at this point, other than to say that things worked out very well for them. We were able to find the right medication to treat the biological component of Tom's depression and, through individual as well as joint therapy sessions, were able to disperse the fusion that had developed in their marriage. Tom and Marsha are much happier today, and both are much stronger for having overcome their ordeal.

BEWARE OF BEING A HURTFUL HELPER: THE CASE OF JANE

Fusion does not always restrict itself just to the venerable and vulnerable institution of marriage, however. Close friends can become fused. Siblings can become fused. Parents and their children can become fused. Any time there's a strong emotional commitment in a relationship, fusion can develop if proper boundaries are not maintained.

When you start to identify the well-being of someone else as synonymous with your own, the danger of fusion exists. Even if the identification is a caring one, it becomes dangerous because you've suddenly put your "eggs" into someone else's basket, and you begin to feel resentful if you don't like the way the basket is being carried. The case of Jane and her mother illustrates this point. Even though Jane loved her mother very much, she wound up feeling resentful and depressed because she allowed her involvement to go too deep.

Jane came to me complaining that her mother had become unbearable since the death of Jane's father. "She calls me up every night and just cries. She wants him back. She tells me she has nothing to live for, that she can't go on without him, that she'd rather be dead. I've tried to help her in every way I can because I love her very much. But nothing has worked. She even accuses me of being insensitive, when all I'm trying to do is help. It's as though she's unloading her depression on me, and I don't know how much longer I can take it. She gets me so upset, and then I start quarreling with my husband. It just doesn't seem fair."

Jane unwittingly had entered the ranks of what I call the "hurtful helpers." She meant well in her attempts to console her mother, but at the same time her resentment at being emotionally drained showed through. She and her mother began to engage in heated arguments, and at one point her mother threatened suicide. This made Jane even more resentful, and their fusion grew worse. Jane had become totally immersed in her mother's depressed world.

"I'm so confused," she told me. "How can I be so furious at someone I love so much? And why is my mother doing this to me if she loves me?"

That's the fate that hurtful helpers face. If you're currently caught in a situation such as Jane's, you know how frustrating it can be. The more you do, the more you do wrong, and everyone suffers as a result. This is because it's simply not possible to solve other people's life problems, or give them the self-esteem they lack, or brighten their spirits when they're dark. By trying to do so, you only risk joining them in their despair—and compounding that despair as a result.

So what *do* you do?

You detach yourself, remain empathic, and set appropriate limits, not coldly or vindictively, but with wisdom and purpose. I'll be explaining precisely how in Part Two of this book, but for the time being let me give you four words that will be useful for you to think about as we begin to look more closely at the fusion process.

▲ *Objectivity*—about your goals and expectations for the relationship
▲ *Knowledge*—about the nature of the depression you're up against
▲ *Empathy*—for what your depressed loved one is experiencing
▲ *Courage*—to face your own inadequacies and reasons for becoming fused with your depressed loved one in the first place

These are the tools you're going to need to help yourself and the depressed person in your life, not pep talks motivated by frustration, and certainly not threats or ultimatums motivated by anger or disgust. Telling someone who's depressed that he or she has pushed you to your limit is tantamount to throwing an anchor to a sinking ship. The depressed person is going to lash out—a sign of just how much more desperate your lack of understanding makes him feel. Even if your helpful advice is motivated by compassion, it will do more harm than good if it does not reflect a very sophisticated understanding of the mental turmoil your depressed loved one is feeling.

REMARKS THAT CAN MAKE A DEPRESSED PERSON FEEL WORSE

You're in extremely touchy territory when you're living with someone who's depressed—the domestic equivalent of walking through a mine field. That's why it's so important for you to learn the right moves to make. Part Two, as I've said, is where we'll be concentrating more specifically on management strategies, but I've decided to offer the following advice now to start you thinking in the right direction. The remarks that you've been making are likely to make your depressed loved one feel not better, but worse, by showing how little you really understand the mental anguish that depression involves. These remarks, well intended and seemingly inoffensive as they may be, can be the kind of fuel capable of keeping fusion ablaze.

WELL-MEANING REMARKS

▲ *"Just know that I care about you and love you."* (Instills guilt and may sharply contrast with other remarks you've been making which show your lack of understanding.)

▲ *"You have so much going for you. You have no reason to feel this way."* (Shows how little you understand what the depressed person is feeling, and also implies that you know more about his or her thoughts and feelings than he or she does.)

▲ *"I'll do anything you want. Just tell me what."* (Shows you're beginning to feel desperate, which can make the depressed person also feel desperate.)

NOT-SO-WELL-MEANING REMARKS (Motivated by Frustration)

▲ *"Wouldn't you feel better if you didn't drink so much?"* (Implies alcohol abuse, which should be dealt with in a less shaming manner. Also misses the more important point of *why* the depressed person may be drinking—to escape inner turmoil.)

▲ *"Doesn't it matter to you that I love you? You never think anybody cares."* (Instills guilt, shows selfishness on your part, and makes the depressed person think he must really be crazy—the result being even greater feelings of hopelessness and despair.)

▲ *"How can you expect to feel good when all you do is sleep all day?"* (Creates feelings of shame, and shows a lack of understanding of how depression can change bodily functions.)

MEAN AND HURTFUL REMARKS (Motivated by Anger)

▲ *"You have no respect for other people's feelings."* (Implies that your loved one is malicious and uncaring rather than depressed. This increases an already overdeveloped sense of worthlessness and isolation, which will come back to haunt you in the form of more despondency and anger.)

▲ *"You love being depressed, don't you?"* (Implies that your loved one is acting and feeling depressed on purpose, which exacerbates feelings of shame that exist already.)

▲ *"You're just out to punish me—why do you hate me so much?"* (Shows misunderstanding of the depressed person's internal conflicts, and significantly increases his already overdeveloped sense of guilt. You are, however, correctly identifying your feeling of being punished—a sign that you're caught in the fusion process.)

▲ *"You're vicious and crazy—stay away from me."* (Shows your anger—which may be legitimate—but also is harshly critical and destructive, which heightens depression and undermines the relationship by increasing fears of abandonment.)

How This Book Can Help

Depression is an insidious illness that feeds on itself and creates an atmosphere that breeds more depression, greater hopelessness, and unending loops of hostility, tension, and gloom. And while we are not born with the intuition or knowledge to deal with depression instinctively, there are specific interventions and attitudes that can maximize the probability of defeating this destructive disorder. I am not talking about mere techniques, however. I'm talking about learning a new way of looking at your loved one, your relationship, and yourself.

In the end, success in life and love is more related to "who you are" than "what you do." Following my program is going to help you better understand yourself, and then use this understanding to your advantage. It's going to help you become better adjusted individually by giving you a more accurate vision of what's going on inside you, and it's going to help your relationship by helping you understand what is going on inside your depressed loved one, and between the two of you. Personal emotional well-being, and maximizing the probability of regaining and maintaining a stable, warm relationship, will accompany these inner and outer changes.

These realities are so clear to me now that I will no longer treat a depressed person without also seeing his partner or family members, for to do so would be to neglect what I now know is a fundamental, treatable aspect of this condition. Through this book, I offer you the knowledge and innovative help that I bring to my patients.

My program is mutually reinforcing in that the very steps you need to take for your personal recovery are exactly the ones that will maximize your loved one's chances of recovery. I say this knowing full well (and reminding you) that no one can cure another person of anything unless that person is willing and motivated. Treating depression requires professional assistance. You can point the way, but you then must get on with your own life. By following the advice in this book, you will be able to:

1. Maintain a warm and caring relationship with your depressed loved one relatively free from the hostility and tension that fusion can inflict.
2. Maximize your loved one's chances of getting well.

3. Learn to cope with the hardships that relating closely with a depressed person can impose.

But first things first. We must determine now whether depression is, in fact, the problem you and your loved one face.

2

WHERE FUSION GETS ITS STEAM: *Depression Can Wear Many Faces*

"These troublesome disguises we wear."

JOHN MILTON, 1608–1661

When I explain the process of fusion to my patients, they usually understand it immediately, especially those who are living with chronically miserable or irritable souls. "My wife sees the world as cold and cruel. She basically feels that there isn't a person out there who cares about her or is willing to give her the love and support she needs. No matter what I say, or how hard I try, it's never enough—she can find a way to turn "I love you" into a put-down. To tell you the truth, there are days when I get depressed the minute I pull into the garage just from knowing what it's going to be like when I go inside."

Other times, depression is much more camouflaged, and

my patients seem shocked when I tell them that the fusion in their lives is being caused by someone who is depressed.

"How can my husband be depressed, Dr. Podell? He's always yelling."

"I thought depression made people mope. My wife is so nervous she has to take tranquilizers to calm herself down."

"Dad's not depressed, Dr. Podell. He's just the biggest bastard ever born."

I get reactions like this all the time from my patients, and what I tell them is what I tell you now: Don't expect depression to produce a sad face only. It can produce as many faces as the people who suffer from it. It can be the face of excitement on the father who is betting the family savings at the track. The face of terror on the teenager who's trying to outrun the police in a stolen car. The face of drunken euphoria on the housewife who's just finished her fourth glass of peach schnapps.

These people are not walking around with their heads down, but they're suffering from depression, nonetheless, and they're causing their loved ones to suffer with them. An estimated thirty million Americans currently are afflicted with an emotional disorder that has depression as a key symptom, and since only one-third of them are being treated, the other twenty million are the people who need to be identified if the contagious spread of depression is going to be stopped.

This isn't to say that all depressions are difficult to detect, however, as we'll be seeing shortly. Serious clinical depression, for example, can virtually immobilize its victims, and manic depression can produce mood changes that are truly frightening. If you're living with someone afflicted with one of these forms of depression, however, you probably know it, and hopefully that person is receiving appropriate treatment.

Yes, you're still going to have your hands full learning to cope with the effects the depression has on both of you, but at least part of your battle has been won. The diagnosis of depression has been made—the "enemy" has been declared.

This is not the case in so many relationships I see, where a mood disturbance exists but has not been diagnosed. These are the depressions I call the great impostors, and though they might not wreak the immediate havoc of more obvious forms of depression, they can do even greater damage over the long haul if allowed to persist. They agitate, they create tension, they breed anger, worry, resentment, and fear. And these are the emotions—not the blatant trauma of having to deal with someone who's had a nervous breakdown—that can so insidiously fuel the process of fusion and cause depression to spread.

"Nice hairdo, honey. Are we really on that much of a budget?"

Funny, sure, but such needling eventually can begin to erode the very foundation a relationship needs to survive. And yes, biting satire, if chronic, could be symptomatic of a depressive disorder. It could be the hidden anger of the "misery-wanting-company" syndrome as the satirist attempts to bring your self-esteem down to a level as low as his own.

"For Christ's sake, have a drink with me. You really don't know how to relax, do you?"

Alcohol abuse, or any substance abuse for that matter, can be a sign of depression as well as a contributing cause. The depressed person turns to the substance as a temporary escape, but then pays a high price in the form of a chemical as well as psychological "hangover" when the escape has ended.

"You take Ben to his recital. I've had a lousy day and I'm going for my run."

Nothing against exercise, but when it gets to the point of becoming an addiction, it can be just as much a coping mechanism for depression as alcohol or drugs. Excessive gambling, eating disorders (overeating, anorexia and/or bulimia), and even excessive devotion to one's career also can be signs of errant attempts to cope with depression.

I tell you these things not to worry you more than you might be worried already, but rather to give you hope. The insufferable SOB in your life may not be such a contemptible wretch after all—he or she may simply be suffering from a treatable mood disturbance. And your relationship may not be doomed to spiral downward into a hopeless cavern of gloom— it may simply be a victim of the fusion process. If your partner were truly mean-spirited, it's unlikely the two of you would have grown close in the first place. It's far more likely that what you're seeing now is a deviation, a change in behavior that has been caused by some treatable psychological disorder.

But people can change with the passage of time, you say? Maybe you and your loved one have simply begun to grow your own separate ways?

We change as we mature, but we don't change our stripes. Most relationships that find themselves deteriorating for no clear-cut reasons have fallen prey to fusion stemming from the contagious emotions generated by a mood disturbance of some type.

Why Feel It When You Can Flee It?

That being the case, it's vitally important that the mood disturbance in your relationship be smoked out, and the sooner the better, because your relationship will continue to deteriorate if it is not. When I told this to Tom and Marsha, the couple you met in Chapter 1, their reaction was typical in that they expressed both relief and concern. They were relieved that there was hope in sight, but they were concerned about how far they'd have to go to get it.

They were lucky, I told them. Marsha had recognized something was wrong in their relationship and came for help in time. They were both a little surprised when I explained the degree to which Tom's depression had been the source of their difficulties, but I told them what I tell all my patients: Depression can cause a lot more waves than those created by its most obvious splashes.

I explained that Tom's displays of anger toward Marsha and the children were attempts to push away the internal pain, confusion, and guilt he was still feeling over severe self-esteem problems as well as unresolved anger at his recently deceased father. The fear that he wasn't going to be able to live up to his father's high standards, moreover, compounded his conflict by creating worry and self-doubt. He wanted comfort and soothing from his family, but he didn't know how to ask for it without appearing shameful and weak. So most of the time he withdrew and sulked until he could bear his anger no more— and then he would blow up. His family couldn't understand this, however, because they didn't know what he was really feeling. They could judge him only by the way he behaved.

What Tom couldn't hide through silence or vent through physical and verbal aggression he was attempting to numb through alcohol. His entire existence, in fact, had become one motivated by his need to flee from the real conflict he was feeling inside. His amazing energy in his job and his obsession with appearing youthful and fit were all part of an elaborate, though unsuccessful, attempt to cope with his internal problems. As long as he could keep from acting depressed, he could deny that he was feeling depressed, so he fought his depression for as long as he could. And yet depression, as we've seen and as we'll continue to see, can do some of its greatest damage when suppressed and denied. The suppression not only allows the depressed person to avoid treatment, but it starts claiming innocent victims as the depressed person begins lashing out at those closest to him. The more a depressed person can create turmoil around him, in fact, the more he can deny that the real turmoil is coming from within him.

"I'm not depressed, I'm simply living in a world that's forcing me to feel worthless and unappreciated." That distorted logic becomes the depressed person's self-deluding rationale, and if you're currently living with someone guilty of such logic, you know how exasperating it can be. You may even have begun to fear, as Marsha began to fear, that the one who's disturbed is you. And you may even have begun to behave in ways, as Marsha began to behave, that make that fear quite warranted.

This is the ultimate danger of living with a depressed person. You begin to "catch" many of the depressed person's symptoms. Whether it's abusing drugs or alcohol, or resorting to violent arguments, or reacting to despondency with despondency of your own, you begin fighting fire with fire and your relationship gets "burned" all that much more in the process.

If you find that you're becoming embroiled in heated confrontations with your loved one, or turning to alcohol or drugs to cope, or becoming uncharacteristically sullen one day and then up the next—all as the result of how your loved one is feeling on that particular day—you're not just a victim of depression, you're an accomplice. You're unwittingly contributing to your loved one's depression by helping to create the very environment it needs to persist, and it's destroying both of you and your relationship along with it.

From Accomplice to Sleuth

So how do you clear the air? Fumigate? Open the windows so your relationship can breathe again?

You've got to stop being an accomplice and start being a sleuth. You've got to stop participating in your loved one's depression and start understanding it. Knowledge is power against depression, not gut reactions or pep talks and certainly not threats. These only foul the air even more by fueling fusion. You're going to have to be objective if you're going to restore the kind of order it's going to take for your loved one to heal, and only by understanding depression can you do that. If you continue to feed depression the emotional conflict it craves, it will grow stronger with every bite.

That being said, it's time to throw depression up on the examination table and see what makes it tick. First we'll look at the masks depression can wear, then we'll pull those masks off and see what's really going on behind them. No two cases of depression are identical, remember, so the more you can understand about the particular case you're up against, the better you'll be able to deal with it. I'll be going into management strategies in far greater detail in the second section of this book, but it's going to help you greatly if you can first understand what you're managing.

Three Shields to the Wind

If you can picture happiness as being dependent on three basic factors—biological predisposition, past experiences, and current life circumstances—you've got a pretty good understanding of what this thing we call depression is all about. If someone is born with basically normal brain psychobiology, even a traumatic upbringing and less than cheery current environment might not cause significant symptoms of an emotional disorder. But if a person's basic brain chemistry is not so hardy, and/or his childhood was not such an ideal one, then a few rainy days could be enough to cause problems.

I'm exaggerating, of course, but only to make my point. Resistance to depression must be looked at as a three-layered shield. If any one of the three layers is thin or cracked, resistance to depression decreases accordingly. This makes some of us vulnerable for biological reasons, others susceptible because of our upbringing, and still others at risk because of current life events.

Any combination of damaged layers is also possible, unfortunately, which weakens resistance to depression even more. It also adds the element of variability to this thing we call depression, as different combinations produce different results. This is why depression can show itself in so many different ways. Except for identical twins, no two genetic predispositions are the same, no two upbringings are really ever the same, and rarely are two current life circumstances the same.

Add it all up and you've got the incredibly individual and yet all-too-common problem of depression that afflicts an estimated one in six Americans today. We all have both natural and learned defenses against depression, but these protective mechanisms are always imperfect—in different ways and to varying degrees. Some of us have such strong biological pre-dispositions that coping mechanisms and background play minor roles in prevention, while others of us have such dam-aged early lives that our coping mechanisms not only fail to prevent depression but actually promote it. Most of the forms of depression we're about to see can be viewed in one of these ways.

LIFE THROUGH THE FISH LENS: COGNITIVE DISTORTIONS

"But wait a minute. My husband actually seems to protect his depression, Dr. Podell. It's not as though he's being vic-timized by a genetic curse or traumatic childhood at all. I be-lieve he continues to be miserable because he actually likes it."

I frequently hear that from patients when I explain my three-shields analogy, but it only illustrates just how deep the effects of a cracked shield can go. If the depressed person in your life seems unable to see his or her behavior for the prob-lem it is, there are "cognitive distortions" going on.

I know that's one of those phrases that can run right by you, but don't let it, because it's a very fundamental problem in many types of depressed behavior. A cognition is something perceived. And we all know what a distortion is. Put the two together and you've got someone simply not perceiving the world as it really is. They see life through their own personal fish lens, and this can be extremely frustrating to deal with, as you may know all too well. Perhaps your depressed loved one is encountering:

▲ All-or-nothing thinking—less than perfection is failure.
▲ Worry that's grossly out of proportion with reality.
▲ Feelings of regret and blame where there needn't be any—but believing that such feelings must be true.
▲ A pervasive sense of guilt—living with "shoulds," "musts," and "oughts."

These are some of the more common symptoms that people with cognitive distortions will display. They overgeneralize, invariably on the downside. They read their own negative thoughts into the words and actions of others. They have their own dark view of the world, which they will cling to no matter how bright things can be.

And the danger, of course, is that these people begin to fulfill their own prophecies. Their negative expectations begin producing negative effects—not just on themselves but on those around them—and this gives them reason to feel even more depressed.

And the cause of this inability to see the world as it really is?

Usually this stems from upbringing—which means that it is something learned and nurtured. People can learn to think in distorted ways due to any number of influences they experience when growing up. Whether someone's childhood was cold and uncaring, physically abusive, or even overly protected, these early experiences can greatly affect the way the adult world is later going to be viewed. It's as though we get the lenses to our cameras focused very early in life. Once set, they can be hard to change.

But others seem to develop cognitive distortions merely as a *result* of being depressed. They might have a weakness in the biological workings of their brain, become depressed for no apparent reason, and then suddenly begin to see the world and themselves as negatively as someone who has been brought up in a disturbed, distorted environment.

I mention all this to emphasize again just how important it is for you to realize how "involuntary" depressed behavior can be. Yes, your loved one may seem to protect or even create his or her misery, but trust me when I say that he or she is not enjoying this misery. Your loved one has become a prisoner of distorted perceptions he or she has become powerless to change. And until you accept that, you will not have the objectivity to do what's necessary to help with the healing process.

That being said, let's look now at the specific forms depression can take. Remember, knowledge is your number one weapon against depression. You've got to know what you're up against before you can defeat it.

NORMAL SADNESS: SUSAN, THE "LONELY MOM"

Susan came to me complaining of a persistent sadness that she said was very inconsistent with her normal cheery nature. She was an attractive woman in her late thirties who had put a successful career as a commercial artist on hold so she could devote all her time and energy to raising her first, and probably only, child.

Things had been wonderful when her daughter, Deborah, was small, but Susan found herself feeling despondent and depressed as Deborah began to mature through early adolescence. Susan was no longer feeling needed by her daughter, which left her feeling empty and alone. Unfortunately, Susan's husband, Sean, responded to Susan's sadness by also becoming upset. If he wasn't withdrawing to his private den to avoid her, he was lecturing her on how important it was for her to return to work as soon as possible. Susan found both behaviors to be insensitive, and this upset her even more. She felt she was being abandoned by both her husband and her daughter. And that's when she came to me.

After determining that Susan was not suffering from a depressive disorder related either to biological or childhood causes—layers one and two of her antidepression shield—I felt confident in advising her on her current life situation. She was going to have to be patient but also practical, I told her. A replacement for the joy she had experienced in nurturing her daughter would have to be found, but she shouldn't feel rushed.

I also assured her that she still had many other joys of child rearing to look forward to—the pride in watching the flower reach full bloom. "You're simply experiencing a normal sadness in response to a major transition in your life," I told her. "Sean is going to have to understand that and stop trying to solve your situation overnight."

Things worked out well for Susan and Sean, as I had anticipated they would. Susan's sadness was not being fueled by underlying predispositions to depression, and she had not been scarred by a traumatic childhood. She merely was going through some of the rough waters that are an unavoidable part of the journey of life.

When I was able to convince Susan of this, she felt much better, as did Sean. She took my advice and worked herself back into her former career gradually, and Sean also took my advice and made his wife's transition easier both by backing off and by taking on more responsibilities around the house. In my last meeting with them, they told me they were as happy as they'd ever been.

I tell you the story of Susan and Sean not to tempt you to overlook what may in your own case be a more serious problem, but rather to demonstrate that it's possible for periods of sadness to occur without depression being the cause. Life is never totally smooth sailing, and sometimes we make the going even rougher if we panic the minute the boat gets the least bit rocky. Look as objectively as possible at what's really going on. Is there a legitimate reason for the sadness or anxiety your loved one is feeling?

If there does seem to be a legitimate reason for the unhappiness, and *no other abnormal behaviors appear to be present*, then a case of normal sadness is probably all you're facing. Just be as understanding as possible in helping to correct the reason for the sadness, and it should pass within a few weeks at most.

And if it does not?

Then you may need to take a different tack. Something beyond normal sadness may be at play. Your loved one may have a crack in one of the other two layers of his or her depression-protection mechanisms—the biological or the cognitive—which is allowing the sadness to penetrate and take root. Not all of us have emotional constitutions that are as rugged as Susan's. The case of Rod is a good example.

ABNORMAL SADNESS: ROD, THE "FEARFUL FIANCÉ"

Rod is a successful physician in his early thirties who came to me at the insistence of his girlfriend, Bonnie. They had been discussing marriage in recent months, but the discussions had started turning into melees. Rod would become defensive and then hostile whenever he felt Bonnie was getting too close—a response, I learned later, that was expressive of the unpleasant childhood he had experienced in a family with two overbearing parents. He was afraid marriage would leave him feeling dominated in much the same way he had felt dominated as a child.

Rod and Bonnie had strong affection for each other, however, so the relationship continued, though "endured" might be a better word. Rod became progressively more disturbed—first hostile, then sullen and withdrawn. This brought out the worst in Bonnie, who would attack him for deliberately trying to sabotage their relationship. This, of course, would sour Rod to the idea of marriage even more. The two of them were like mountain goats with their horns locked, neither being able to make a move without angering the other—a classic case of fusion.

More important for our purposes here, however, was the nature of Rod's depressed behavior. It was similar to Susan's in that Rod was reacting with feelings of distress to a current life event (i.e., the prospect of marriage) that he found upsetting. Yet it was unlike Susan's, given the weaker coping abilities that Rod carried against this upsetting circumstance.

Rod had been scarred by his childhood in ways that Susan had not, so his behavior wound up representing concerns of the past as much as the present. This is a very common occurrence with people whose childhoods have been difficult. They react to current life events in ways that really represent unpleasant remembrances of their pasts. Tom, in Chapter 1, as you'll recall, became abusive and turned to alcohol in response to his dwindling self-confidence and the unresolved guilt he felt for never having come to peace with his harsh, abusive father. Rod, in a similar way, was becoming depressed at the prospect of marriage due to the unfavorable relationship he had experienced under two dictatorial parents.

I tell you this to help you find what may seem to be some missing pieces in the disturbed behavior of a "Rod" in your life. It's very possible that a rocky upbringing is responsible for some of the current instability you're seeing in your loved one. His or her behavior could be the result of concerns about the past as much as the present.

Depressions of this type are extremely common but also quite treatable with psychotherapy, fortunately. Once the depressed person is made aware of the hidden forces influencing his or her behavior, there usually is a sense of discovery and relief that becomes the beginning of a more rational view of present events.

In Rod's case, the discovery led to very good things indeed. When we pinpointed his childhood relationships and family role as the core of his problem, marriage seemed less threatening, he was better able to relax with Bonnie, and she was better able to relax with him. Their sense of safety increased, intimacy developed, and they finally were able to set a date for their wedding after weathering a long struggle with these disturbing, contagious feelings.

"I'll show up if you will," Rod joked as he handed me a wedding invitation one day in my office. And I can vouch for the fact that Rod spread very positive emotions to everyone he touched at the celebration. He had come a long way.

WHEN THE GENES ARE DEPRESSED

If you're getting the impression that we're moving in a direction of increasing severity here, you're correct. We're looking at the mildest forms of depression first—those with the smallest number of contributing factors and also the least intense contributing factors. Susan, as an example, experienced only a normal sadness in response to her stressful life event because she brought no genetic predispositions to her sadness, nor was it compounded by any unpleasant flashbacks of a damaging childhood. Rod, by comparison, was less equipped to handle his stressful life event because he was haunted by memories of a burdensome upbringing. It's time now to see what can happen when psychobiological susceptibilities begin entering the picture.

DYSTHYMIA: LORRIE, THE MISERABLE "DOUBLE DEPRESSIVE"

Lorrie is one of those people who might be described as only slightly more upbeat than the Grim Reaper. If something isn't wrong with her, there's something wrong with the weather, the economy, her furnace, her dog, or her car. People like Lorrie are special in that so much ails them from the inside that almost anything can ail them from the outside. They suffer from a type of chronic depression we call "dysthymia." This kind of depression is so much a part of their lives that they seem to have "depressive personalities" more than depressive episodes. They simply seem down all the time.

Lorrie came to me after I first had been visited by her husband, a man who, understandably, appeared about as chipper as Dracula at sunrise. Nothing was ever right for her, he told me. When he once had tried to cheer her up with a new car, she complained about the color. "She could find a dung heap in paradise," he told me in total despair.

When I finally got to meet with Lorrie, I asked her how long she had been feeling depressed, and her answer didn't surprise me. "All my life," she said matter-of-factly. She went on to tell me about how her mother had been chronically depressed, and how her father had been cold, moody, and highly critical. She told me she had felt unloved as a child and that she had been overshadowed by a vibrant and beautiful older sister.

She had been very unpopular as a teenager, a loner who had run away from home several times and who had even contemplated suicide. It all came to a head during her sophomore year in college, when she experienced a major depressive episode in response to breaking up with a boyfriend. She pulled out of it about six months later without undergoing any treatment, but she went on to fluctuate between periods of mild and severe depression from that point on.

What makes people like Lorrie so glum?

Usually it's some fairly serious damage to their sense of self, as a result of a difficult upbringing. This results in poorly developed coping strategies and destructive, distorted perceptions of themselves and the world in which they live. But there can also be biological factors that contribute to this tendency toward depression.

In fact, Lorrie had a biological susceptibility to depression, which she had inherited from her depressed mother. She also had a less than cheery childhood, which left her feeling worthless, fearful of being unlovable, and chronically angry. These two predispositions to depression—early-life psychological trauma and biological susceptibility—combined to produce a personality ripe for depression no matter how trauma-free her adult life might turn out to be.

Lorrie was lucky in that she married someone who not only was able to keep her comfortable financially, but also was able to be reasonably understanding. Had her adult life turned out to be less accommodating, she probably would have been even more incapacitated by her depressive tendencies.

I'm still treating Lorrie and her husband, so I can't yet give you a happy ending to their story. We are making progress, however, and we're doing it through the strategies I'll be explaining in Parts Two and Three of this book. So please, keep your chin up if you're living with someone who's as chronically miserable as Lorrie—someone who can see the cup as half empty even when it's running over. There's still hope.

The important thing to remember with people like Lorrie is not to let their misery pull you down, too. Yes, it's natural to want to "save" a person who suffers from chronic depression because he or she appears to be drowning, but trust me: There will be no rescue by you alone. Those who remain untreated will continue to drown until they can be made to throw off the emotional shackles of their depressed childhoods and learn to "swim" on their own. In some cases, accomplishing this may require medication to manage the disordered brain chemistry that helps cripple their ability to think, act, and feel normally. Many of the same challenges hold true for people who suffer from another form of chronic moodiness known as "dysphoria."

DYSPHORIA: RICHARD THE TERRIBLE

People who suffer from dysthymia are a burden to live with because they're down all the time, but people who are dysphoric can be even tougher to deal with because they can be up and down like a roller coaster—sullen at times, but highly agitated at other times.

"We just never know what to expect, Dr. Podell. Richard can be quiet and even sulky one minute, but then get angry and abusive over almost nothing. It's extremely hard on me, but I think it's even harder on the kids."

Those were the words of Richard's wife, Carol, the first time she came to see me. Pretty quickly, I had an idea of what we were up against. Richard also drank quite heavily, used cocaine when he could get it, and was legendary for his high-rolling wagers on the golf course—one of which had won him the use of a friend's Porsche for a full year. He also, however, had cost the family its summer vacation one year by losing the rights to its beach house.

"That's the way he is, always looking for some kind of action to keep his mind occupied. He seems so unsettled, so angry, so tense."

Carol was describing dysphoria to a T. Its sufferers are at such odds with themselves and so unable to endure their own emotions that they'll try almost anything for relief. They'll drink too much, smoke too much, use drugs, binge on food, become addicted gamblers, even engage in inappropriate sexual sprees—anything to divert them from facing the fears, conflicts, and feelings of emptiness that exist within.

Yet the sad reality, of course, is that these behaviors usually only compound their problems. Whatever biological, childhood, or situational factors may be contributing to a dysphoric's internal fires in the first place, the coping strategies they adopt only fan the flames. In Richard's case, his abuse of alcohol and cocaine would provide him relief temporarily but leave him with even more self-disgust when they had worn off. His gambling sprees would do the same. He'd feel great when he'd win—but like sheer hell when he'd lose.

And taking the brunt of it all, of course, was his family. The worse Richard felt about himself, the harder he was on Carol and the kids. "If he loses on the golf course, I just grab the kids and go to a movie," Carol told me. "You get out of the way of the steamroller when he's like that, or you get crushed."

We'll be looking more closely at cases of dysphoria in the management section of this book, because not only is it one of the most hurtful types of mood disturbances to live with, but it's probably the most contagious. People who are dysphoric tend to exhibit self-destructive behavior as well as behavior that is abusive to others, a combination that treats fusion to a veritable pipeline of high-octane fuel. Arguments often begin over one of the abused substances or one of the impulsive or compulsive behaviors that are being used as a substitute for healthy coping. "If I say as much as a word about his drinking or gambling, he's through the roof," Carol told me. "He guards those things with his life."

If you can identify with Carol, rest assured that you're in good company: Dysphoria is one of the most common types of mood disturbances. Also be assured, however, that I'll be giving you very specific strategies for dealing with this highly destructive form of moodiness in Part Two of this book. Yes, dysphoria is a monster to live with, but the monster will continue to run wild if its underlying causes are not tamed. I'm not suggesting that's your job, however. As we'll be seeing, that work belongs to a mental-health professional.

CLINICAL DEPRESSION: "RITA'S REACTION IS MORE
THAN JUST GRIEF"

So now we're ready for the big stuff—the major depressions, the heavy hitters that knock their victims flat and leave them for near dead. These depressions are going to be unmistakable, right? As obvious as the face that can't find the pride to shave, much less leave the house to go to work. Or the waves of tears that come daily, for no reason. Or the suicide note.

Don't be so sure. Major depressions do not always cry out so loudly for help. They can, like the lesser forms of depression, camouflage themselves in other behaviors. Or, as in the case we're about to see, they can be obscured by their association with other tragic life events.

Rita and her husband, Matt, had been trying to conceive their first child for a period of four very trying years. Rita had even undergone a major operation to clear her fallopian tubes. But tragedy struck less than three months after the joyous news that Rita and Matt had succeeded in fulfilling their dream. Rita miscarried in her eleventh week, and she was shattered. Matt was able to get over his initially very extreme grief within about two weeks, but Rita was not.

Rita would cry at the sight of pregnant women and other people's babies. She couldn't regain the energy to return to work, she began having trouble sleeping, her appetite was down, and she lost weight. She even began losing her overall zest for life, and was haunted by thoughts of suicide. Rita's gynecologist thought she was merely going through a "grief reaction," a response to her tragedy that would pass. Friends consoled her by saying that she was "just going through a tough time." However, I wasn't so sure.

Matt had come to me approximately three months into his wife's "grief reaction," and after hearing all her symptoms I had to tell him I thought something beyond normal grief might be going on. Rita was presenting with many of the symptoms of serious "clinical" depression, which is not just an emotional disorder but a biological one in which the brain does not function as it should.

Matt told me that two of Rita's grandparents had been seriously depressed, one to the point of requiring electroconvulsive therapy, so the pieces seemed to fit. Neither of Rita's parents had suffered from depression, and while Rita's childhood had been a normal and even warm one, that was not sufficient reason to rule out a biological cause for her depressed state.

"But wouldn't Rita have experienced signs of her illness prior to this episode?" Matt wanted to know.

Not necessarily, I told him. Her biological predisposition for depression may never have been activated by any previous life events or stresses because of her good coping strategies. But the prospect of never having a baby may have overloaded her psychological defenses and created brain-chemistry changes capable of pushing her into her current depressed state.

Subsequent meetings with Rita revealed that her grandmother on her father's side had been ill to the point of requiring hospitalization in a psychiatric facility. I won't give you the details, but realize that if a person came to the attention of the psychiatric community in 1935, there was a good reason. Rita had never thought much about her grandmother's depression, however, because "it had been so long ago."

Time affords little protection from this type of depression, however. It's possible for some clinical depressions to hurdle not just one generation, but several—something to keep well in mind if you're currently living with someone whose persistently dark moods don't seem to make sense. Clinical depression, like a hidden virus, can rear its ugly head at virtually any point in a person's life span if the person is carrying the biological potential. Sometimes it takes a trigger, like the tragedy Rita experienced, but many times it does not. If you suspect that clinical depression may be plaguing someone in your life, by all means look closely at the following list of key symptoms. If, in addition to a depressed mood, four or more of these symptoms are present *every day* for a period of *at least two weeks straight*, clinical depression is probably what you're facing.

CLINICAL DEPRESSION: KEY SIGNS

▲ Sleep disturbances (too little or too much)

▲ Appetite disturbances (increased or decreased)

▲ Decreased ability to concentrate

▲ A distorted, highly negative, or pessimistic attitude

▲ Excessive feelings of guilt and/or low self-esteem

▲ An inability to experience pleasure

▲ Low or absent sexual desire

▲ Excessive fatigue

▲ Psychotic thinking accompanied by delusions and/or hallucinations

▲ Suicidal thoughts or attempts and/or preoccupation with death

▲ A diminished ability to function at work, at home, or at school

---

As devastating as clinical depression can be, however, be assured that some extremely effective therapies are now available. We'll be examining those therapies in detail later in this book, but for now please know that clinical depression is a very serious and potentially even fatal condition that should be treated as early as possible. Roughly fifteen percent of the people who suffer from serious clinical depressions will, in fact, take their lives if not treated in time.

MANIC DEPRESSION: RAYMOND, THE "ROCK STAR"

Patricia had not been in my office more than five minutes before she burst into uncontrollable tears.

"I've never been so afraid, Dr. Podell. When Ray's like this, he's just a totally different person. His eyes are so wild, it's like they're not even his. And his thoughts are so crazy. He's telling me now that Rod Stewart has been trying to get him to be the drummer in his band. He's never even met Rod Stewart, Dr. Podell.

"But the worst part is that I never know when he's going to become violent. He can be so happy having his wild thoughts, but if I say one thing wrong he begins to act like he's going to kill me. I'm afraid he's going to hurt someone when he's like this, or get hurt himself. Can't we get him into a hospital where he'll be safe?"

Patricia was experiencing the horror of living with a manic depressive going through a manic phase. Ray was lucky to get an hour of sleep a night, and would go several days without eating. But worst of all were his totally irrational fantasies—not just Rod Stewart wanting him to join his band, but the novel he was writing that John Updike was going to help him get published, and the acting career that Ryan O'Neal was going to help him launch.

If you would go along with Ray's fantasies there would be no problem, but question any of them, and you were taking your life in your hands. More than once, Ray had seriously injured people in barrooms after some fellow drinkers had found his grandiose schemes hard to believe.

And yet as wild as manic depressives can be on the high side of their cycles, they can dip to near suicidal despair when in their lows. Ray would sleep for twenty-four hours at a stretch and sometimes gain as much as fifty pounds. He couldn't function at his job as an automobile salesman and would "just vegetate at home," Patricia told me. "It's as though he's only half alive."

Granted, Ray had a serious, poorly controlled case of manic depression, but even milder forms can be very difficult to live with, as the element of uncertainty always lurks. When's the "good" mood going to turn bad? When's the bad mood going to turn into a "high?"

Manic-depressive cycles can vary in length as well as degree of severity. One form of the illness known as "hypomania" is actually considered to be quite pleasant, some patients tell me, because its highs often do not reach a point of being un-manageable. Even with hypomania, however, there is always a risk of escalation to more severe forms of the illness, so while this variation of the illness is more mild, it still must be treated by a professional. Hypomania also can be hard to live with, as irritability is a frequent by-product of its uncommon energy.

What causes manic depression, and what are the best treatments?

The illness is thought to be biological and hence inherited in most cases, but there have been instances of manic depression occurring in people with no evidence of the illness in their families. As for the best treatment, medication therapy is proving to be extremely effective in over two-thirds of cases. Psychotherapy is also very important, because most manic depressives tend to deny the severity of their illness and often refuse to take medication properly.

It is almost impossible to live with or relate closely to an untreated or partially treated manic depressive without having high levels of anger and frequent arguments. So let me say for

now that if you think manic depression may be affecting someone in your life, professional care is going to be required. The
illness will exasperate you as much as the person suffering from
it, and your relationship, and maybe even someone's life, could
be the ultimate price.

DEPRESSION IN CHILDREN: BAD KID OR SAD KID?

Depression is certainly not limited just to young or middle-
aged adults. It can occur in children and the elderly, as well,
and it can be a source of fusion, accordingly.

"He's run away twice. He's doing terribly in school. He's
sulky, he's disrespectful, and I have reason to believe he's
smoking pot at night in his room," Chuck's father told me.

It was a classic description of a depressed child. Depressed
children frequently do poorly in school, reject social activities,
spend a great deal of time alone in their rooms, and may even
run afoul of the law. Such behaviors rarely get recognized as
symptoms of depression, however, which tends only to make
the depression worse.

"I make him toe the line," Chuck's father told me when I
asked him how he responded to his son's difficulties. "He's
only 15 and he's acting like a goddamn criminal. He's driving
his mother and me nuts."

Here was fusion "family style." Chuck's misbehavior, which
was due to an underlying depression, was causing his parents
to fight, which was making his depression worse. Every domestic skirmish would give further support to his view of life as
cold and harsh. Every marine-sergeant ultimatum from his
father would confirm his view of his parents as uncaring ty-
rants.

If you're the parent of a child exhibiting delinquent behaviors such as Chuck's, please remember to at least consider
that a treatable psychological problem may be responsible.
Children suffer from many pressures parents are not aware of.
And they also can be prone to depression for reasons that are

biological. They need, in short, to be given the same psycho-logical respect as adults. Have your child see a mental-health professional with special training in child psychology or psy-chiatry if you suspect a depressive disorder may exist.

Depression in the Elderly: The Senility That's Not

Depression in the elderly can be especially unfortunate, because it frequently gets misdiagnosed. If an older person begins to withdraw and have trouble thinking and commu-nicating, senility is often assumed to be the cause when depres-sion may actually be the problem. I could offer many examples, but let's look at Ann, whose case was an especially dramatic one.

Ann is a woman in her 70s who had been labeled as suffer-ing from Alzheimer's disease and sent to a nursing home for "long-term maintenance." I was asked to give Ann a psychiatric examination, and I came up with a rather shocking discovery when I did. I believed that she had been misdiagnosed and that she was not suffering from Alzheimer's at all, but rather a severe clinical depression that had significantly slowed her mental processes.

Many doctors, let alone family members, do not realize that severe depression in elderly patients can cause such profound changes in thinking. Memory impairment, extremely poor con-centration, confusion, fearfulness, even psychosis (including loss of reality, hallucinations, and delusions) can result from a depressive disorder.

I began treating Ann with Desyrel, an antidepressant medi-cation, and within several weeks the nurses told me she had become a "new person." She was talking, laughing, holding complex conversations, and asking when she might be going home. Needless to say, it would have been a great tragedy had this proper diagnosis not been made.

Treating "pseudodementia," the depression masquerading as senility, with antidepressant therapy continues to win us great praise as many patients return to being highly functional people. So please—if there's a loved one in your life whom you suspect may be senile, have him or her undergo a psychiatric evaluation. You could possibly save him from a very sad fate if you do.

DRUGS, ALCOHOL, AND DEPRESSION: BEWARE OF THE CHEMICAL HANDCUFFS

Do people use drugs and alcohol because they're depressed—or do drugs and alcohol cause depression?

The answer to that question remains a somewhat controversial one, but a verdict does seem to be emerging: It depends on the person. I have successfully gotten patients off drugs and alcohol by treating their depressions, and I have successfully treated people's depressions by getting them off drugs and alcohol. Every user uses for different reasons.

There is no question, however, that alcohol and most drugs—cocaine, especially—can promote depression through their pharmacological effects on the brain. Thus it only makes sense to encourage a depressed person to discontinue alcohol or drug use when the goal is to improve his or her life outlook.

I recently had an outstanding success with this approach in the case of Steve, a middle-aged TV producer who was so depressed—and drinking so heavily—that his career was about to be canceled. He had been to several different psychiatrists and had tried many different antidepressant medications, with no success.

What did bring him success, however, was when I talked him into entering an alcohol-detoxification center. Once I had him off the booze, I started treating him with Norpramin, an antidepressant, and the medication was able to work. It was proof of just how powerfully depressing alcohol can be.

Yes, Steve was suffering from a depressive disorder in addition to being depressed by his heavy intake of alcohol, but it was the combination that was proving so devastating. He was throwing rocks onto an already sinking ship. Now that Steve's drinking is behind him, he's a "brand-new man," more vibrant, witty, energetic, proud, and hardworking than he's ever been in his life, because his depression no longer weighs him down.

I also have had similar successes—though ones harder won—against cocaine addiction. Even if a depressive disorder is the reason cocaine is being used in the first place, the disorder becomes far more treatable once the cocaine use has been stopped. In those cases, it usually is necessary to use antidepressant medications to bring such cessation about.

The bottom line is that mood-altering substances such as alcohol, cocaine, amphetamines (and I include heavy marijuana usage, too) may seem to provide escape from depression in the short run, but in the long run they just raise the prison walls higher. Bear that in mind as we begin discussing the specific strategies it's going to take for you and your loved one to escape whatever form of depression may be gripping you. All chemical handcuffs are going to have to be removed if you're going to set yourselves free.

The Gender Crunch

Before concluding this chapter, we need to address one last, very pertinent fact: Depression afflicts women at twice the rate it afflicts men. Lopsidedness like that cannot be explained away by chance.

Several factors may be responsible for the difference. The intense pressure women feel in trying to be both a breadbaker and breadwinner; the difficulty in maintaining high self-esteem despite what continues to be widespread male chauvinism; female hormonal tendencies toward depression as exemplified by premenstrual syndrome and postpartum blues; and finally, the stress-producing tedium of household duties, which women continue to bear more than men.

Making these burdens even worse may be the recent pressure from the feminist movement to make changes. Sociological change takes time, but not many women are being led to believe they have the time to make such changes.

I mention this because it needs to be taken into account by all couples who may be struggling in their relationships. If you're a woman living with a depressed man, realize that any one of the above factors may be adding to your plight. And if you're a man living with a depressed woman, realize that these factors—in addition to whatever more "medical" causes may be at play—may also be taking their toll. Do not assume than she's free of the real stresses of life just because she's not the primary money-maker. Research shows that the role of housewife, precisely because it *can be* uneventful, is among the most stressful occupations of all.

So should all bored wives of the world just go get jobs?

That solution, unfortunately, misses the point. Research shows that the greatest stress producer of all is a feeling of subservience, of perceiving a lack of control over one's life. Unless your wife could assume a position that would bring her a higher sense of dignity than she's getting at home, it's unlikely that joining the work force would improve her subordinate feelings or change her dim view of her life.

Conditions *are* improving for women, but slowly, unfortunately, so men and women alike are going to have to be especially sensitive to current inequities as long as they prevail.

But enough theory. We've seen the various faces depression can wear, and we've taken a look at what can cause these faces. Now it's time for the all-important matter of how these mood disturbances can spread to those who come into contact with them.

3

How Fusion Does Its Harm:
It Takes Two

"Force without wisdom falls of its own weight."

Horace, 65–8 b.c.

We've looked at the different faces depression can wear, and at what can cause depression. But now it's time to focus on you. We're going to be examining how depression can spread, and yes, you play a very important role. There's truth to the old saying that "it takes two to tango," after all.

The process we'll be examining is what I've been calling "fusion," a phenomenon very similar to the type of fusion that exists in the world of nuclear physics. Just as the interaction of two atomic particles can create vast amounts of destructive nuclear energy, interactions between you and your depressed loved one can create great amounts of destructive *emotional* energy.

47

Relating closely to a depressed person will likely cause you to experience anguish and turmoil that will rob you of self-esteem, optimism, your capacity to love, and your ability to enjoy life in general. I'll be instructing you on how to prevent and counteract this fusing process in the second section of the book, but for now I want to be sure that you fully understand how damaging—and often difficult to recognize—the fusion process can be. Consider the case of June as our first example.

For fifteen years, June lived with a man who never could find anything right about anything. The house was never big enough, the bills were never small enough, his shirts were never white enough, and the grass was never green enough.

June was born and raised in the Midwest, and was a hard-working college-educated woman who was trained as a nurse. She was basically a very positive person, but in time she found herself becoming almost as negative and faultfinding as her husband, Sid. Sid was a quiet, stern man, a pharmacist by profession and a workaholic by anyone's standards. Not only was his mood chronically depressed, but he was very irritable and thin-skinned. June would find herself complaining to him for complaining so much, which would only make him more irritable and likely to complain even more.

Their relationship had become "fused"—locked in a mutually harmful cycle, whereby negative attitudes from Sid would produce negative attitudes in June. Many relationships endure this sort of "not-so-merry" merry-go-round for years, and many even survive it, but always a high price is paid.

In June's case, even though her husband eventually was cured of his depressed ways of thinking, she was left as a victim. All the years of emotional drain had left her tired, confused, and empty, so empty that when her husband finally did get well, she found that she was emotionally scarred herself. Her husband had escaped his depression, but not before passing it along to her! This is the very real danger of living with a depressed person. Unless you keep a healthy emotional distance, you will suffer psychological harm.

But wait a minute. If you love someone, you should stick by him "in sickness and in health," right? Even if it means fighting and risking some wounds yourself, the important thing is to show you care.

Wrong. Here is where millions of well-meaning people set themselves up for needless misery. It's a misery, moreover, that winds up doing far more harm than good for the person it's intended to help. Your greatest obligation to a depressed person is to avoid joining him in his woes, which is exactly what will happen if you get lost in the fusion process. And once you start to share the depressed thought patterns of your depressed partner, you will plummet further as a team.

It never fails to shock my patients when I tell them that sympathy and feelings of obligation "to love and obey until death do you part" are not the ways to deal with a depressed person. Only by *staying* well can you help a depressed person *get* well, and only by knowing how and when to keep your distance can you do that and thus be truly supportive.

June's husband was lucky. He found good professional help and got well, despite his wife's involvement in his depression, but not before it was too late for June. Had June known how to deal with her husband years earlier, his depression might not have progressed to the point it did, and June would not have suffered to the point she did.

But no, June let her feelings of obligation and her emotions be her guide, and the process of fusion pulled her into her husband's depressed world as a result. Depression may be the enemy your loved one faces, but the process of fusion is the enemy you face. Let's take a closer look at exactly how fusion works.

Misery Demands Company

You've just completed a two-hour bus ride with someone whose main topics of interest all have seemed to start with the letter "d": death, disease, divorce, natural disasters, the federal deficit, and drugs. How are you going to feel?

You've just heard your beautician tell another horror story about either her finances, her fiancé, her Fiat, or her aching feet. How are you going to feel now?

Like it or not, it is human nature to be affected by the emotions of the people around us. This can be good when the emotions are positive ones—such as the mass excitement experienced at a sporting event or the laughter shared among friends over a good joke—but it can be very bad when the emotions are negative ones. Moreover, the bad effects extend beyond just making us share the same ill feelings as the person experiencing these negative emotions. When we begin to share the negative emotions of another person, we begin to act differently toward that person, and here's where the destructive force of fusion begins to gather steam.

When confronted with the hardships or pessimistic thoughts of another person, it is a natural reaction to feel a threat to your own sense of well-being. This extends from the instinct we all have for basic survival. Sure, you feel bad about your haircutter's latest car bill, but at the same time you can't help feeling a little angry that she brings you down, too, by sharing it. Like a bad cold, it's a shame if somebody has one, but that doesn't mean you're going to be happy if they go sneezing in your face. You're going to be especially unhappy, moreover, if this "sneezing" person is someone you must confront every day of your life!

That, in greatly simplified form, is the core of the problem in having to live with a depressed person. Any close relationship—but marriage especially—takes this "please don't sneeze on me" phenomenon and magnifies it thousands of times over. It simply is not fun to live with a negative person, and it is only natural that you will feel resentment if you are made to do it.

Even if you are not conscious of this resentment, you are going to feel it. Worse yet—and here's where the trouble begins—you're going to *show* it. Whether you know it or not, your own need for well-being will defend itself when confronted by a depressed person and you will protect yourself usually un-consciously, in ways that the depressed person will detect.

Not Such Idle Threats

But let's slow down for a minute. Why should resentment be so inevitable when you are living with a depressed person? Can't you have the compassion and reason to be kind and caring without feeling such resentment and, worse yet, show-ing it?

In most cases, no. And as ironic as it sounds, the closer you feel to a loved one, the worse your chances of succeeding at hiding your resentment are likely to be. This is because your closeness is a big part of the reason you find your loved one's behavior so threatening in the first place.

Threatening?

Yes, threatening. Your loved one no longer provides you with the feelings of warmth, security, and safety that were major reasons for your attraction to him or her in the first place. Now he or she is disturbed, erratic, sometimes passive, some-times aggressive, sometimes abusive, sometimes weak. He or she is not living up to what you thought your relationship would be.

And harsh as it may sound, part of you feels cheated. You feel you've been sold a bad bill of goods. And if you hear talk of his or her leaving the relationship, or suggesting that you leave, or—worse yet—of wanting to commit suicide, you really feel shortchanged. Now an element of out-and-out fear enters the picture. You find yourself in a situation—and yes, a threatening one—that is highly uncomfortable and certainly not what you had expected your relationship to be.

Adding to your fear and sense of being cheated is apt to be yet another hurt: a serious blow to your self-image. Why has your loved one become so disturbed? Just how instrumental a role have you played? Could it be your fault? And why haven't you been able to be more helpful? These thoughts can pose very real threats to the image you would prefer to have of yourself.

And who's to blame for the threats? That's right. Your "loved one." The person you're supposed to be feeling sorry for. This person used to make you feel good about yourself, but now his or her abusiveness, or lethargy, or lack of pride and perhaps even slovenly appearance have you thinking that maybe you're a loser, too.

So how are you going to respond to these threats?

Whether you're conscious of them or not, and whether you know it or not, you're going to strike back. As hard as you may try to be patient, caring, and helpful to your loved one, your resentment and self-protective mechanisms are going to show through. Why is your loved one doing this to you? You did nothing to deserve it. You feel an injustice, and whether you know it or not, your feelings are going to reveal themselves. Let's look at the case of Jim and Terri as an example.

Jim has been married to Terri for over ten years. She has suffered two major depressions in her life, and has been depressed on and off for a period of six years. On this particular evening, Jim comes home somewhat upset after a rough day that has given him reason to worry about losing out on an important promotion. Terri is sitting on the couch, and Jim can see just from the look on her face that she's in one of her more depressed moods.

This immediately makes him feel nervous, so he extends nothing more than a reasonably cordial hello and begins to pace around the room. Sensing it's going to be "one of those nights," he goes into the kitchen to start dinner, then comes back into the living room to watch TV but can't find anything he likes. That's when Terri unloads.

"You're driving me nuts," she shouts. "You can't sit still for a single second! You're so irritating. No wonder I'm so depressed!"

Jim, understandably, attempts to defend himself. "I could see that you were in a bad mood when I came home so I was trying not to bother you. I even started dinner. I can't take it anymore. You're the one who's screwed up, not me."

Terri, of course, holds her ground. "If you could see I was feeling bad, why didn't you sit down and try to talk to me? But no, you just pace around because *you've* had a bad day. You're just too damned self-centered, Jim. No wonder I feel so depressed. I'm all alone."

Bad Vibrations

What you've just seen is fusion in action. The fusion started with Terri's nonverbal communication of her depression to Jim, who then reacted negatively by feeling intensely nervous as well as understandably resentful about the unpleasantness that he knew the rest of the evening would bring. Terri quickly picked up on Jim's anxiety, which pulled her mood even lower, and whammo: Terri "lost it" as the fusion of her depression with Jim's anxiety produced a case of psychic overload she couldn't contain.

Who's "to blame" here?

On the surface, it would seem to be Terri. But after seven years of this sort of thing, Jim probably knew what he was doing. He was expressing his resentment over his wife's condition. He perceived his wife's unhappiness as a threat, so he sent out signals that would make his feelings known.

If you were to ask Jim, as I did, if he meant to upset his wife, he would say he did not. And he'd probably be telling you the truth. But the human psyche often acts independently of human awareness. Jim, without knowing it, is developing pronounced emotional problems and mood disturbances much like his wife's, and he's beginning to exhibit distortions in his powers to think and behave logically as a result.

This is the natural and inevitable consequence of living with a depressed person. You literally begin to "catch" the depression yourself, because your own sense of well-being gets eroded as you struggle with the conflict that the depression imposes. You want to be helpful and caring, but you also want to protect yourself. And what happens, unfortunately, is that you lose yourself in the process.

This is perhaps the most dangerous aspect of the fusion process. You become so involved in your depressed partner's world that you begin to lose touch with your own. Everything you say or do becomes a *reaction* to what your partner says or does. You may even pull away from your normal activities and your normal circle of friends as you lose *yourself* more and more. Just as with nuclear fusion, in which two atomic particles become one, you and your depressed partner become one. You begin to lose your boundaries. Who's the one who's depressed? Whose anxiety is whose? Who has the problems? Who's the "crazy" one?

Those questions get harder to answer, unfortunately, the longer fusion goes on.

The Failure to Communicate

So your loved one's depressed behavior—whether it's reclusive or abusive—poses threats to you. And it's only natural for you to react in ways that show your resentment of those threats. Jim's reaction was to become silent, nervous, and fearful, but he might just as well have shouted at the top of his lungs that he was sick to death of living with a lunatic. His behavior communicated the same message to his wife.

So why doesn't Jim just come clean with his wife? Spare the cat-and-mouse game and let his true feelings be known?

For the same reasons you haven't. You may not know your true feelings, first of all, but you may also be afraid of the consequences of speaking them. Your main concern, after all, is that your loved one get well. And that makes sense, because if he or she does get well, you feel all your troubles will be behind you. So you walk softly. You try to be supportive. You try to arrange events that will help your loved one buck up. You do everything you can to make the depression go away.

But guess what. You may only be making your loved one's

depression worse by behaving this way. My patients always find that hard to believe, but it's true. As you try to "massage" your depressed loved one, it's inevitable that he or she will sense the real desperation that you feel, and he or she will be further alienated and depressed by the insincerity that your "soft touch" conveys. Your light-handed approach also may make your depressed loved one feel even more like a "cripple" than he or she already is.

Is this to say you should tell your loved one like it is, come hell or high water?

Not quite, but I'll be getting more specific about that in Chapter 5. For now I want to make sure you understand the way the mixed messages you may be sending your depressed loved one are aggravating more than soothing his or her condition. Your intentions, on the surface, may be good. But down deep you're feeling a need to defend yourself against what you are quite correctly perceiving to be a threat to your own mental stability.

You're putting forth what I call "incongruent communication," words that are saying one thing but actually meaning another. This type of communication happens very often when people attempt to deal with depressed persons, and it is perhaps the most "active ingredient" in the fusion process.

You'll no doubt recognize the following types of incongruent communication if there's a depressed person in your life. And remember: If you're guilty of these faulty forms of communicating, you probably are not aware of it. Part of you is feeling genuinely sympathetic and caring, but another part is feeling violated and trapped. The result is a dishonesty in what you say and do—a dishonesty that your depressed loved one will detect and interpret as intentionally hurtful or uncaring on your part.

THE NO RESCUE RESCUE

Unlike the "let the sleeping giant lie" approach that backfired so badly on Jim, the "no rescue rescue" is characterized by an attempt to be overly helpful. You make efforts to leap into your loved one's troubles with both feet, only to wind up knee deep in quicksand for your efforts. Consider the case of Mel and Sally as an example.

Mel is a carpenter in his mid-50s whose wife, Sally, has been depressed for about three years. She works as a sales manager at a local department store and has a 22-year-old son by a previous marriage with whom she has a troubled relationship. Mel loves his wife and wants to be as helpful to her as he can, but when it comes to sitting down and patiently listening to her problems, he becomes noticeably anxious.

"Mel, I feel lousy," Sally announces one evening after a harrowing day. "My supervisor at work is getting on me again. She's complaining that business is down and that my department's figures aren't as good as last year's. I tried to explain that the new line they bought just didn't sell, but she wouldn't hear it. My son has been calling, too, asking for money again. At first I said no, because I know I shouldn't, but he sounded so desperate and made me feel guilty, so I wound up mailing him $200."

Mel responds quickly. "Why don't you just tell your boss to screw off? You work your butt off for that store. I think you should quit or ask for a transfer. You've got to make them stop pushing you around. And as for your son, he's been using you, too. He's the biggest manipulator I've ever seen. All he does is freeload off you and then give you a lot of headaches. I think you should tell him to stop calling until he gets a job. I hate to see all these people taking advantage of you, honey. You've got to start sticking up for yourself, and I'm here to help you do it."

Mel rests his case, expecting Sally to be thankful for his support. But no such luck.

"You don't understand me at all," she shouts. "You don't know what goes on at work and you don't understand my son. You'd just love it if we didn't see each other at all. You really hate him, don't you?"

Mel is at first speechless, but not for long. A shouting match quickly ensues that wounds both parties deeply. Where did Mel go wrong?

Mel's "solutions" to Sally's problems did not represent adequate thought, and Sally could tell. Like Jim, whom we discussed earlier, Mel feels very uneasy around his wife when she begins to act depressed, but unlike Jim, who clams up, Mel opens up. What he often dishes out, however, rarely reflects his true feelings, which are frustration and fear much more than the cut-and-dried confidence he attempts to convey through his knight-in-shining-armor facade.

Sally senses this "incongruent communication" from her husband and responds by feeling frustrated herself. In the shouting match that ensues, both Mel and Sally go on to galvanize distortion and animosity rather than get to the bottom of their misunderstanding. They become two more victims of the truth-ruining fusion process.

Undercutting

Undercutting is a form of incongruent communication more apt to be used by your depressed loved one than by you, but its effects on your own abilities to communicate can be just as harmful to your relationship as if you were guilty of undercutting yourself. This is because living with a chronic undercutter makes you become overly protective of your true feelings, the result being that your undercutting partner begins to become just as suspicious and mistrusting of you as you become of him. It's yet another variation on the fusion theme. Let's take a look at the "undercut" in action.

Hank is a successful stockbroker in his fifties who has had several bouts of depression during particularly stressful times in his life. His wife, Lorraine, is basically a very loving person who cares about her husband, but when he undercuts, she stabs back.

"Hank, I've found a piece of real estate that I think is a really great buy. It needs work, but I just know it can be a gold mine with the right renovations. I've got some terrific ideas for it and can't wait to get started. What do you think?"

"I think you should check other prices in the area first. A good friend of mine just got burned because he didn't know how to research his place's real value and bought on impulse. He also got nailed by trying to be his own contractor. One of his subs wound up being a crook who took him for over $10,000."

Lorraine reacts hotly. "What are you trying to say, Hank, that I'm a stooge? I told you about this place a few weeks ago and you said it sounded like a winner. Weren't you listening? Probably not. You never listen, unless it's about you. Are you afraid I might actually make some money here? You treat me like an idiot, just like you treat the kids. You just love to sit around and cut us to shreds."

Hank retreats, but only for the purpose of altering his attack. He acts surprised, but continues to support his point of view as he contends that he meant no harm. This, of course, only angers Lorraine further, because in addition to having her competence undercut, she's now being told she "heard things incorrectly." The two of them part ways as classic victims of the fusion process.

If you share a relationship with someone who communicates in this "undercutting" style, you know how hurtful it can be. Worse yet, you may be left wondering which of you is, in fact, correct. There's so much gray area that you feel lost in the fog. The two of you are arguing over whose interpretation of reality is closer to the truth, but the truth gets harder and harder to find because of all the "smoke" created by your argumentative fires. This is a very serious and destructive situation, which must be extinguished if either of you is to see the light.

LOSING THE BULL BY THE HORNS

This third form of futility in dealing with a depressed person can be especially exasperating, and if you've made the error, you know. A loved one's depression can be like a bar of wet soap in that the harder you try to take it into your own hands, the more it's apt to slip away. Overly aggressive attempts to control a depressed person's unacceptable behavior are only likely to magnify that behavior, as the depressed person usually will react very defensively as a way of denying that he or she has problems. Worse yet, your efforts are apt to be viewed as vindictive rather than caring, which will add further confusion and conflict to your fused relationship. Consider the case of Paul, for example.

Paul is a screenwriter and one of the seven children of two alcoholic parents who, despite less than diligent life-styles of their own, expected great diligence from their offspring. This left Paul with a role but no role model; depressed behavior in the form of addictions to everything from alcohol to exercise was the result, as Paul would attempt to numb himself in any way possible to his multitude of internal confusions. If he wasn't overeating, he was starving himself. And if he wasn't high on alcohol or pot, he was high from a torturous bout of exercise.

Paul's wife, Karen, was a very stable and caring person. After one too many years of Paul's "insanities," as she correctly called them, she decided it was time to play tough. She burned his pot, threw away his wine, shredded his exercise suit, and carted his entire cabinet of health food off to a local institution for the homeless. She even set up an appointment with a therapist.

And how did Paul react?

Within twenty-four hours he had things back to "normal" and then some. He greeted Karen at the front door as she returned from work the next day wearing two sweat suits, a hash pipe in one hand and a glass of champagne in the other. On the stove was a cabbage, lentil, and oat-bran stew.

Depression, Karen learned, is not a disorder that responds well to being pressed for a cure. The word itself should give you a clue: de-"press"-ion. The depressed person already feels "pressed" enough by the demons that haunt him. He or she does not need additional pressure, even if it's from a well-meaning loved one, to make those demons go away.

What happened to Karen is a critically important aspect of the fusion process. She lost her boundaries. She became so obsessed with Paul's addictions and mood disturbance that she began to deal with them as if they were her own. And in a sense they had become her own. That's how much she had lost herself in her husband's world. Her problem was that she was living with an emotionally disturbed man, but she didn't understand it that way. She saw his problems as her problems. Eliminate them, and everything would be great for both of them, she thought.

But she had it quite wrong, unfortunately. Paul felt understandably violated by Karen's actions, which allowed him to focus on her rather than the real issues—i.e., his addictions—which were in much greater need of his attention. This was a case of fusion being so blinding that it forced both of its victims to live in the dark.

Fusion Eruptions

We've seen how the process of fusion can cause depression to be "radioactive" in a sense by making depression harmful just to be around. This is because a depressed person poses threats to you, threats that cause you to react defensively despite your wishes to be helpful. This in turn confuses, frustrates, angers, and further depresses your partner, and an emotional interplay very analogous to a nuclear reaction gets set in motion.

Energy is released—very negative and hurtful energy—which can leave both of you injured, and angrier than ever. And as your partner's depression gets worse because of these destructive exchanges, the more frequent and destructive the exchanges will be. You will find yourselves the victims of what I call "fusion eruptions," those catastrophic blowups that raise the roof and leave both of you first livid, then numb, then more hateful than ever. What triggers these catastrophes? Is one of you more to blame for them than the other? Why do they make you do and say things you inevitably regret?

An eruption recently reported by two patients of mine might shed some light. Harold and Margo have been married for thirty years, but not very happily. Margo had a very militant father who terrorized the family with his vicious temper much of the time. Like her mother, Margo would remain very passive in the face of her father's outbursts, finding this the most effective way of dealing with his rage. This personality style continued into Margo's adulthood and characterized her interactions with both Harold and their two children, Lisa and Mark.

Harold also grew up with an abusive father and passive mother, but Harold's reaction was to fight back when his father would attack, an aproach that also would persist into his adult life. Harold always felt as though he were in a life-and-death struggle with everyone around him, Margo and the children included. Harold started experiencing episodes of depression in his late 20s. Margo could always tell because he would begin to drink too much, have difficulty sleeping, and also become more irritable than ever. It was during one of these depressed periods that the following "eruption" between Harold and Margo occurred.

Harold asked Margo to give him a haircut. He had an important business meeting the next day and wanted to look his best, but he had been too busy that day to go to his usual barber. Margo had been giving the children haircuts for years, so Harold felt in no great danger of being scalped.

But scalped he was. Or at least in his estimation he was.

"Jesus Christ," were his words as Margo held a mirror for him to see the back of his head. "Do you think I'm headed for the fucking marines?"

Harold went on to accuse Margo of attempting to sabotage his chances for success not just in his meeting, but in his entire career. She was "jealous and resentful" for having to stay home with the kids, he said. She was "losing confidence" in her own appearance and becoming "fearful" that Harold was beginning to see other women. "You've tried to fucking castrate me here," he shouted loudly enough to wake both the kids.

And that ignited the bomb. Margo, too, exploded. She told Harold that he was a self-centered, faultfinding, uncaring, insecure son of a bitch who was failing miserably as a provider, a husband, and a father combined.

This, of course, further opened the floodgates for Harold, who went on to blame Margo's "over-mothering" for everything from his own problems to 10-year-old Lisa's continued bed-wetting. And around and around they went until the scissors were waved and the mirror was smashed.

The rest of the evening was a case of nuclear fallout, as the children cried themselves to sleep, Margo stayed up all night weeping, and Harold spent the evening between the local taproom and the lounge chair in the garage. Let's examine, blow by blow, how this fusion eruption came to be.

Round One: *Provocation.* The act of provocation in this case was Margo's decision to cut Harold's hair shorter than he wanted. Did she do it intentionally? Probably not. But she probably did do it subconsciously as a display of her repressed resentment over Harold's disagreeable behavior and lack of respect for her domestic role.

Round Two: *Escalation of Anger, Stage One.* As Harold expresses his anger over Margo's provocation—one which he perceives to be clearly deliberate—she responds with even greater anger at feeling falsely accused. She also feels an element of having been "caught" for what, on a subconscious level, she did mean to do, which makes her even more animated in her anger by adding a factor of defensiveness to her wrath. This makes her "hit below the belt" with remarks that attack Harold in what she knows to be his most vulnerable areas. Her remarks extend far beyond the scope of the argument at hand, but she feels justified because Harold has attacked her in her most sensitive spots.

Round Three: *Escalation of Anger, Stage Two.* Harold defends himself by expanding his attack on Margo's greatest vulnerabilities—her uncertainty regarding her responsibility for his depression and their 10-year-old's problem of wetting the bed.

Round Four: *Violence Brought on by Frustration.* In this case nothing serious transpired, but many times serious harm is inflicted. Margo simply wielded the scissors and smashed the mirror, but she could have done far worse. Her actions were violent enough to signal a victory for Harold, however, because she had acted as the "crazier" of the two.

Such unfair "victories" demonstrate just how harmful fusion eruptions can be. They resolve nothing and distort the truth. Harold clearly is the less mentally stable partner in this relationship, yet he emerges from this skirmish as the less disturbed of the two. His relationship with Margo and his depression, as a result, take one very giant step backward from where they need to go to get healed.

The Consequences of Leaving Bad Enough Alone

So that's fusion, in all its ugliness and pain. Depression may be the problem your partner faces, but fusion is the problem you face. It will infect you with your loved one's depression if you do not learn to stop it, and it will worsen your loved one's depression in the process.

"But won't this fusion thing finally just go away if I'm patient and try not to become so upset?"

I frequently get asked that question by people who find themselves in fusion's grip, and I tell them very honestly what I tell you now. Fusion, in most cases, is like a brushfire in that it will burn until it has nothing left to consume if the problems creating it are not resolved.

Only in families where healthy relationships exist prior to the onset of a depression will the depressed person instinctively protect his family members by withdrawing and shielding them from his depression. This buys time and keeps fusion at a lower level so that minimal turmoil is created before the depression can be treated. This allows loved ones to be far more supportive, caring, and helpful.

This is not true, however, in relationships that are troubled prior to the onset of depression. In these relationships, a depressed person will inflict his bad feelings and frustrations on those closest to him. This, of course, ignites the fusion process, and it can be very hard to stop if the necessary interventions aren't made early enough.

Worse yet, fusion can begin to damage relationships to the point where they become irreparable even after the depression has been cured! Your formerly depressed loved one may act totally normal around others but *remain* in a fused state with you. This is why some relationships appear to become hopelessly "dysfunctional." Years of fusion have created wounds that become almost impossible to heal.

Fusion and the Family

But the dangers of prolonged fusion stop not just with the two warring parties directly involved. Everyone associated with the feuding gets hurt, children especially. The consequences of growing up in a family undergoing fusion can be as devastating as growing up in a family being torn by the abuse of alcohol or drugs.

Research shows that over 60 percent of children brought up in households where depression has caused conflict will, in fact, wind up with serious psychological problems. I hope that statistic has a sobering effect on you if you're currently involved in a seriously conflicted relationship with your spouse.

If you have children, start observing them. How are they taking it? And don't dismiss any possible connections: Hyperactivity, bed-wetting, despondency, school problems, drug abuse, and even problems with the law all can be signs that the children are being unduly upset.

You must realize that children are different from adults in that they usually express their feelings through actions rather than words. This can add to the conflicts you're already having with your spouse, unfortunately, as smaller fusion fires spread and create more negative emotional arousal, which makes fusion's main fire burn even hotter, but it's important to realize these "sparks" for what they are. Your children are being upset by what's going on just as much as you are.

The effects of fusion on children give me all the more reason to urge you to act, and act soon, if you feel you and your spouse may be caught in fusion's web. If your attitude is one of, "But it's our problem, no one's suffering as much as we are and we'll work it out our own way," you could be subjecting your children to unneeded harm. It's *not* just your problem—other people *are* suffering as much as you, and no, you probably won't work it out in your own way. That's the reality of your situation that you must come to accept.

I made this point to Harold and Margo in a recent session (you'll remember them as our highly volatile haircutting couple mentioned earlier in this chapter) and both, surprisingly, agreed that it was likely that children could be traumatized by a troubled marriage. I say surprisingly because Harold and Margo, as you'll recall, had children of their own—a girl and a boy, ages 10 and 6. Couldn't they see what their fighting was doing?

Yes, but in the heat of battle they would forget. Both Harold and Margo agreed with tears in their eyes that they owed their children the right to feel secure, and yet their roof-raising melees would still occur. I made it clear to them that this was proof of just how uncontrollable and blinding the rage caused by fusion can be—and how important it was for them to learn to stop it.

Yet the children's problems often provided a welcome focal point for them, something to distract them from their own problems and a place to point fingers and falsely explain their own misery as a reaction to unruly, disturbed children.

No Generation Gets Spared

I saw an opportunity to make yet another point, and an equally important one, in this session with Harold and Margo. "What do your parents think about your current difficulties?" I asked. "Do they even know about them?"

And of course they knew. Harold's father, albeit with the help of a half a fifth of scotch, wept one night regarding his son's troubles. "I think he feels partially responsible," Harold said. "He used to fight just as violently with my mother. But he still doesn't fully understand his part in my problems. He makes things worse, in fact, by making negative comments about Margo. He and Margo barely speak—and that's when things are good between them."

"Who tells Margo about these negative remarks?" I quickly asked.

Harold stuttered and said, "Well, I guess I might have shared a few with her. But I told her I thought my father was being unfair."

Harold had dragged in his father's feelings as a way of expressing his own. And the result, of course, was that he added even further to the troubles he was having communicating with his wife. He also further soured the already bitter relationship that Margo and his father had.

Harold's mother, now divorced from his father, was equally upset by her son's failing marriage. "I never know what hour of the night she's going to call," Harold told me. "I think I'm as woried about her as she is about me."

This concern was hardly shared by Margo, however, who

referred to Harold's mother as "an upper-middle-class bag lady, a manipulative and meddlesome witch" who still had Harold tied to her apron strings.

It was all too clear just how wide Harold and Margo's fusion had spread. Three generations were being affected. Who could say how many more would be affected if Harold and Margo would not stop the fire once and for all?

My point to Harold and Margo was simply this: The fires of fusion burn all. No generation gets spared. And if you want to step outside the family structure and look at friends and co-workers, you'll find that they, too, are feeling the heat.

Harold confessed to me that close friends of his had become extremely concerned about his situation, and Margo told me the same. Harold's office mates could tell when he'd been in a recent fracas, and the wise ones would hold their peace. Others, however, would offer words of "advice," usually in the form of "get rid of the bitch." Such remarks would only pull them into the fusion fire, however, when their hostility would be returned through Margo or one of her friends carrying an equally angry message for them. Fusion's fumes pollute far and wide.

It's Codependency Any Way You Slice It

Codependency has become a much-used and perhaps even overused term, but awareness of the problem has been a great help to millions of people who have found themselves trapped in the sick lives of others. As much as has been written about codependency, however, understanding fusion can give even greater insight into this widespread problem.

Codependency is a natural reaction to being exposed to the contagious emotions of a psychologically disturbed person or family system. You become codependent by instinctively responding to the emotional threats that you feel are being imposed on your well-being. When this happens to you as a child, you learn to accept a role that keeps you safe—a role that has you trying to please the sick people around you as a way of coping.

Living with a depressed person can do the same thing! If the disturbed behavior caused by your loved one's depression has become the central concern in your life, you have fallen prey to this very dangerous pitfall of the fusion process. Just like the codependent of a drug addict or alcoholic, your moods and your actions are being controlled by the moods and actions of your depressed partner. You may even feel that you are powerless to experience the happiness you long for unless your partner gets well—again, a sign that you have become dangerously dependent on your partner's well-being for your own.

This bondage must be broken, for your sake as well as for the mental health of your partner. Only by achieving freedom from this unhealthy dependency can you create the environment it's going to take for your loved one to acknowledge and deal with his troubles as they really are.

You may think you're helping this person with your angry, hard-edged confrontations and outbursts, but such unproductive confrontations are only providing your loved one's disturbed behavior with the kind of camouflage it needs to survive. Nor is rolling with the punches the answer, because it leaves you bruised, feeling inwardly angry and worthless, and it gives your partner the impression that he can continue the barrage because deep inside you really don't care.

So what's the solution?

Now that you're finally informed of the problem, it goes as follows.

PART

TWO

The Prescription for Change

HOW TO DEFUSE, STEP ONE:
Managing Yourself

"First keep the peace within yourself, then you
can bring peace to others."

THOMAS À KEMPIS, 1380–1471

But enough bad news. Yes, depression is an all-too-common disorder that can spread to anyone who comes in close contact with it via the process of fusion. But the good news is that depression can be treated and fusion can be stopped. No matter how hopeless your situation may seem, it can be improved. You might even feel encouraged if your situation seems hopeless, because it means you're going to be that much more motivated to employ the corrective strategies I'm about to recommend. Sometimes it takes being at the end of your rope before you can see that it's time to start climbing back up.

"But I've got to be honest with you, Doctor, I'm not even sure I want this relationship to work out. I've been through so much and hurt so badly that *any* change seems attractive. I've run out of options and patience, too."

I encounter that reaction frequently from patients, and it's a very natural one. You're exhausted from the fighting, the frustration, and the pain. You long for an escape. You crave to be free!

And you can be. That's the unique aspect of the plan I'm about to unfold for you. In addition to helping breathe health back into your sick loved one, it will help breathe health back into *you*. It can help you regain the confidence, strength, and feelings of independence that your relationship with your depressed loved one has drained. Even if things don't go well and your loved one does not get better, you'll be on your way to having a happier and more rewarding life of your own.

I call this "can't lose" aspect of my program the Three-Way-Win. By following the plan presented in these next three chapters, you will be able to:

1. Stop the fusion process and hence the destructive turmoil that's ruining your life.
2. Maximize the chances that your loved one will achieve recovery from his or her depressed state.
3. Sufficiently get your own life back in order so that you can be happy even if your depressed loved one does not get well. You also will be better prepared to deal with life if you decide your relationship with your loved one must be ended.

The plan is divided into three parts—Managing Yourself, Managing Your Loved One, and weighing the benefits each of you could derive from Seeking Professional Help. We'll be looking at the latter two parts in Chapters 5 and 6, but first and foremost our focus is going to be on managing yourself. Not until you learn to be less "flammable" is your loved one going to stop throwing matches. More than you may realize, how you react to your loved one's disturbed behavior can be influential in whether or not he or she gets well. I see it over and over in my practice. If a patient is resistant to treatment, it's often because his or her depression is being rekindled each week by emotional struggles that are occurring at home.

That's why it's going to be important for you to pay close attention to the "defusion" strategies in these next two chapters. By managing yourself in the ways I recommend, you will be creating the environment best suited for helping your depressed loved one get well. You also will be safeguarding your own emotional health. So let's not waste any more time. Let's see what this all-important process of "defusion" is going to require.

STEP ONE: ACCEPTING RESPONSIBILITY

There are several stages to the defusion process, but the first and most important is accepting responsibility for the role that *you* are playing in the relationship problems you're having.

But wait a minute. Your partner is the one who's sleeping until noon, or gambling away the family savings, or talking about suicide—and yet you're supposed to worry about the part *you're* playing in these troubles?

That's right, and if you can learn to think of fusion as a game of tennis, you'll see why. Both of you are hitting accusations, resentments, or threats back and forth, and blaming the other each time such volleys occur. And yet, if one of you would simply stop returning the ball—and I suggest it be you—the volleys will stop. This isn't to say your loved one is immediately going to stop "serving" his disturbed behavior at you, but by refusing to react angrily to this behavior, you'll at least be bringing an end to the back-and-forth battering that has been creating the fusion in your relationship.

No problem? Compared to going tooth and nail with your partner, a policy of turning the other cheek should actually be easy.

It's only fair to warn you that it may not be. If you're like most of the patients I treat, you'll find yourself confronting three formidable forces that will be exhorting you to continue in your warring ways. These forces are guilt, anger, and fear.

The guilt will come from a very natural feeling that by refusing to struggle with your partner, you're abandoning him. You're selfishly leaving him to tangle with his tortured soul all alone. The guilt may loom especially large if your loved one is not aggressive and abusive so much as passive and forlorn. How can you disengage from someone in such a helpless state?

You can because you *must* if you really want your partner to get well. That might seem hard to believe, but you must realize that your loved one stands to gain nothing from being pa-tronized. Nor will he gain from being harangued. You must accept that your loved one's depression is a disorder that will need a period of being "quarantined" to stand its best chances of being resolved.

This is especially important to bear in mind given force number two that frequently keeps people fused with their depressed mates—fear. By continuing to focus on the problems and inadequacies of your loved one, you may be covering up for fears you have of dealing with problems and inadequacies of your own. We'll be seeing this in several case histories shortly, but let me say for now that fear of this type can be a powerful force in keeping you involved in your fused struggles with your loved one. The fusion "protects" you from acknowledging that you have weaknesses of your own, that you may lack the abilities, emotionally as well as professionally, to make it if your relationship were to end. You may even have begun to *blame* your partner for your feelings of inadequacy. His depression, after all, is what has kept you at your wit's end. How could you be expected to function at 100 percent considering the stress you've had to endure?

That question brings us to the third and perhaps most formidable force of all that's keeping you fused with your loved one: anger. You're angry for the burdens you're being made to bear. Your life is being taken away from you by the concern you're being made to feel for your loved one, and it's filling you with a resentment you can't hide. There are times you wish your partner had never come into your life.

If any of this is hitting home, don't feel bad. The guilt, fear, and anger that I've been talking about are very natural reactions to having to cope with someone who's emotionally unwell. The illness creates a crisis, the crisis creates upsets, and it's very natural to respond to these upsets with the guilt, fear, and anger we've just discussed.

A crucial point needs to be made here, however. *You do not have to act on these feelings.* You *must* not act on these feelings, in fact, if your partner is going to stand his or her best chance of getting well. To do so will only perpetuate the fusion process that has been contributing to his problems in the first place. This is the responsibility you must accept. You must realize that the ball is in your court when it comes to stopping the destructive emotional exchanges that have been bringing such pain and despair to your life.

STEP TWO: RESPECTING THE POWER OF PEACE

When I say that you must start taking responsibility for your end of the fusion process, I'm not suggesting that your loved one's behavior has not been legitimately upsetting. But let's not forget what we've learned about the signs and symptoms of most depressive conditions. They not only change the way a person feels but actually distort the way a depressed person is able to perceive, and hence respond to, the world. This means your loved one may be feeling, thinking, and acting in ways that are no more within his control than coughing is within the control of someone suffering from pneumonia. So why torture yourself—and your loved one, too—by taking his sick thoughts and actions so personally?

That should be a fundamental point to keep in mind as you find yourself wrestling with the day-to-day challenge of maintaining your cool in the face of your loved one's provocations. Yes, you're going to want to react emotionally, but to do so will only increase the hostility in your relationship and increase the likelihood of more provocations coming in the future. Turmoil only encourages more turmoil when you're dealing with someone who's depressed, so your goal must be to start calming the raging waters.

Some of the strategies you're about to learn may initially feel more like acts of surrender than steps toward victory, but if you'll just be patient, I guarantee you'll experience positive results. What you're going to be doing is changing your tactics and starting to play it smart rather than tough. You're going to be replacing force with finesse, and if you can think of your loved one's depression as a wound that gets pulled open wider each time a skirmish occurs, you'll see why these peacekeeping strategies can work.

You may think you're having a therapeutic effect when you let your true feelings be known by blowing your stack, or think you're being caring by stuffing your anger, but you're actually only making your loved one's condition worse by causing him to defend himself or to feel demeaned. Your attacks also allow your loved one to believe that *you* are the disruptive force in the relationship and the cause of his depressed moods. This does nothing for you except further entangle you in fusion's web.

But someone's got to put your loved one in his place, you say? How else is he going to get the message that he's wrong, that he's hurting other people, and that he needs to see his depression for the psychological disturbance it really is?

That's my job, or the job of some other qualified health professional. Yes, your help is going to be needed in getting your loved one to seek professional care in the first place, as we'll be seeing in Chapter 6, but it is *not* your job to pass psychological judgment. Your opinions will not be accepted by your loved one, because they'll be held suspect as due to selfish and hurtful motives. Not until all tension and hostilities are cleared from the air are worthwhile lines of communication between you and your loved one going to be possible.

STEP THREE: OVERCOMING ANGER

A lot of emotions can feed into the fusion process—fear, guilt, worry, resentment, jealousy, disgust, and even love—but the end result is almost always anger. Fusion is like a blender, in that no matter what emotions go into it, anger is what comes out. Sometimes the anger is silent and sometimes it's shrill, but it's always anger, nonetheless. This anger then produces more anger, and fusion is off on its unmerry way. I've seen couples in my office begin to argue over issues as seemingly inane as a butter dish being left out of the refrigerator overnight, and yet once battered by the blades of fusion, the issue of that butter dish becomes shrapnel capable of cutting straight to the heart.

The first step to controlling fusion, therefore, is to control anger, and while you may not be able to control your loved one's anger, you *can* learn to manage your own. I'm not saying you must learn to control the feelings that make you want to express your anger in the first place, because many times those feelings will be justified. What I am saying, however, is that anger is apt to be your least effective means of seeing to it that the issues *responsible* for the anger get properly addressed.

Consider the case of Maureen as an example. I was treating her husband, Marty, for chronic anxiety and depression. He had depressions that were accompanied by episodes of extreme irritability; and yet as ill-tempered as Marty could be, he would complain to me constantly about his wife's short fuse. It was not unusual for their quarrels to result in shattered dishes and visits from the local police. "She can go absolutely nuts," Marty told me.

Fully aware that the pot was calling the kettle black, I asked to see Maureen anyway, because I knew her fighting was all the wrong medicine for her equally excitable husband.

"But how else am I going to get through to him? He doesn't listen unless I yell," was Maureen's first reaction when I explained that her blowups were only aggravating her husband's condition and making her own situation worse by fueling fusion.

I decided to answer Maureen with two questions of my own. "How do you feel when your husband becomes enraged? And how does it affect the validity of what he's trying to say to you?"

"I feel threatened, and I stop listening because it makes me realize how out of control he is," was her reply.

And with that, I rested my case. Maureen was falling into a classic fusion trap—the "volume wars," where less gets heard the louder the voices get raised. I explained that if Maureen really wanted to get through to her husband, she'd have a much better chance by doing it calmly. By becoming enraged, she was only conceding credibility with every decibel her voice would rise. Nor was becoming sullen and withdrawn the answer, because it would only make her feel, as well as appear to Marty, that she had accepted defeat. Maureen was going to have to learn to manage her anger rather than letting it control her.

But in the heat of battle, that's just about impossible, you say?

Challenging, maybe, but not impossible. If you find yourself facing an enraging situation, there are calming techniques you can employ. These techniques are not intended to have you denying that you *feel* angry, but rather stop you from *acting* angrily. To attempt to deny your anger would be to violate all the psychological rules for maintaining inner peace and sound mental health.

What we're talking about here is learning to manage your signs of *anger arousal*—the red face, pounding heart, and sizzling language. Research leaves little doubt that anger arousal puts a serious damper on the ability to think rationally, so you must learn to view it as fusion's best friend.

ANGER-CALMING STRATEGIES

▲ *Learn to feel anger coming.* Only in extreme cases does anger come without warning. Usually you'll notice that your breathing becomes fast and shallow, your pulse quickens, you feel a tightness in your stomach, and your muscles become tense. When you feel these sensations beginning, simply discontinue the conversation that's arousing you, and remove yourself from the presence of your loved one if need be. Don't storm off or leave sulking, just say, "I'm becoming too upset and will discuss this later."

▲ *Learn to call for a time-out.* Even if you can't catch your anger in time and you find yourself in the midst of a fracas, learn to leave the skirmish before too much damage gets done. Remarks such as, "Let's stop, we're fusing," or "I'm too upset to talk rationally" can provide an appropriate cutoff.

▲ *Don't be afraid to talk to yourself.* Many of my patients find it helpful to be able to listen to a peacekeeping voice inside them that simply says, "Time to calm down, you're losing it," when their emotions begin to run too hot. Learn to keep an ear open for this voice, and heed it.

▲ *Try to be objective about what's angering you in the first place.* As I've said before, your loved one may not be totally in control of the behavior you find so upsetting, so try to keep that in mind when provoking situations occur. This isn't to say you need to approve of your loved one's behavior, but it will be helpful if you can at least remind yourself that it's being caused by a disturbance beyond your loved one's ability to manage.

▲ *Try to pinpoint why you feel angry.* This may not be possible until you remove yourself from the anger-provoking situation, but it can be helpful in preventing future battles. The better you can understand what your loved one's words and actions touch off in *you,* the greater your sense of control is going to be.

▲ *Get physical.* No, I'm not talking about fisticuffs, I'm talking about exercise. If you've removed yourself from a quarrel and you're still steaming, put the steam into something healthy like a walk, jog, bike ride, or whirlwind cleaning of the house.

Please remember the goals of my anger-management strategies. They're intended to keep you from adding anger arousal to an already overloaded situation. By employing these strategies effectively, you'll be refusing to ride your end of the fusion seesaw, which will leave your irritable, depressed loved one sitting in the dirt with no one to jump up and down about but himself.

This is precisely the kind of emotional isolation he or she may need to experience before being able to acknowledge his disturbed state. The isolation will require that you, too, be prepared to endure some emotional distance and loneliness, but this is the temporary sacrifice you must make if you and your loved one are going to be able to put your relationship back on an even keel. (See the Bibliography for additional reading references on anger-management skills.)

Avoiding Fusion Sparks

Besides learning to manage your anger, it can be helpful to know what makes you angry in the first place, and as much as I've seen couples fight over everything from infidelity to finances to whose job it is to clean up the pet droppings, I've found that most eruptions are ignited by some fairly standard "sparks." You should learn to recognize these sparks, and then refuse to be ignited when they come your way. You also must do your best not to go emitting any of these sparks yourself.

ANGER-CAUSING STATEMENTS

▲ *Statements That Blame* ("If you weren't such a neatness freak, I wouldn't feel so uncomfortable in my own home.")

▲ *Statements That Instill Guilt* ("You work so much that these kids are being raised just like children of divorced parents.")

▲ *Statements That Threaten Abandonment* ("You've gone too far this time, I just can't take it anymore.")

▲ *Statements That Make Charges of Inadequacy* ("You're really screwed up. You just don't know how to love someone, do you?")

ANGER-CAUSING ISSUES

▲ Family members being criticized
▲ Accusations that either of you enjoys the turmoil you find yourselves in
▲ Accusations of insensitivity, selfishness, and/or meanness
▲ Accusations of sexual disinterest or dysfunction
▲ Disagreements over who can do what with the family earnings, and why
▲ Debates over the "right to know" where either of you goes and what you do
▲ Quarrels centered on destructive behaviors such as drinking, drug use, gambling, workaholism, overeating, or compulsiveness

You and your loved one may have other issues of contention, but I'm going to guess that you have one or more of the above as well. Learn to recognize these issues for the troublemakers they are, and do your best to avoid raising them in the predictable ways that cause anger arousal to flare and fusion to flourish.

Your goal should be to keep the peace, because a peaceful environment, as difficult as it may be to achieve at first, will extinguish the fusion and help your loved one see his depression more clearly. It's also going to help you concentrate on your own needs rather than on just those of your ailing partner. As you'll see in the next chapter when we discuss limit setting and confrontation, keeping the peace does not mean absorbing punishment, insults, or tolerating dysfunctional behavior, but it does mean managing your anger arousal.

But remember that more than just anger is pushing you to stay fused with your partner. You also may be feeling the influences of two other powerful forces—fear and guilt. Let's see how these can be tamed.

Step Four: Overcoming Guilt

Beth, a 40 year-old artist, was a patient of mine whose husband, Marv, a 42-year-old lawyer, was not only depressed but was an abuser of alcohol and drugs. Their relationship was a veritable barbecue of turmoil, as she would berate him constantly for his actions. She also spent a great deal of energy hiding his problems from his business associates and friends, yet she told me she could never leave her husband, because it would be wrong to "abandon" him in his obviously disturbed state. Nor could she bear to have their daughter undergo the psychological trauma of divorce. "I'd feel guilty for the rest of my life," she told me.

I went on to explain to Beth that guilt is a very common and natural reaction to the kind of emotional disengagement that defusion strategies require. You may feel you're abandoning your loved one by disengaging from him and you may worry that the disengagement will give the impression that you don't care. However, just the opposite is true. You must disengage from your loved one precisely because you *do* care. You must realize that your guilt is giving you all the wrong messages. It's encouraging you to continue to embroil yourself in your partner's problems in ways that may only be providing fusion with additional heat.

The important thing to understand about guilt is that while it can appear to be a rational emotion, it usually is based on fear, and acts as the emotional "glue" between people who are involved in troubled relationships. If you are motivated to behave in a caring manner through guilt, this guilt is not a healthy bond between you and your loved one, but an unhealthy one. It is preventing you from allowing more rational feelings to prevail.

Beth's feeling of wanting to stick by her husband and feeling terrible about the notion of her daughter going through life with divorced parents *seemed* like justifiable concerns to her. Yet the truth was that her husband was spending the family's money on drugs, creating tension in the home, and relating to his daughter in a highly dysfunctional, disturbed manner. Guilt had blinded Beth to these harsh realities.

Overcoming guilt is no small task, yet it must be done. Under my guidance, Beth came to learn that her guilt feelings would not simply go away. Antianxiety medication helped ease her tension and provided some relief, but the rest had to come from acting with the understanding that her guilt was as unjustified as it was unhealthy. Her guiding light was my voice always asking, "What would a well-adjusted person without guilt feelings do in your situation?"

She seemed always to know the right answers, and I urged her to follow her intellect and accept the reality that while *acting as if the guilt did not exist* would intensify the guilty feelings in the initial phases of defusing, the guilt would eventually fade away to nothing more than a flicker of discomfort.

Step Five: Overcoming Fear

Another difficulty many people have with the defusion process is overcoming fear. They subconsciously fear that if they stop focusing on the inadequacies and problems of their disturbed loved ones, they'll find themselves faced more directly with inadequacies of their own. Staying focused on your depressed loved one can also help you avoid facing the possibility that your relationship may no longer have any passion, or that you and your partner no longer have visions of life that are compatible. You may find it easier to leave bad enough alone and stay angry, rather than stand up by yourself and face the reality that your relationship is in need of help.

If you suspect that such fears may be at work, all I can tell you is that nothing stands to be gained by this kind of bondage. Only losses will occur. Yes, you may feel alone and afraid as you begin to detach yourself from the emotional struggles that have kept you bonded, but eventually you will find yourself able to grow and be happy in ways that otherwise would not have been possible. Consider the case of Lindsey as an example.

I began meeting with Lindsey after first meeting her husband, Adam, a successful businessman in his early 50s who was suffering from a chronic depression that produced recurrent periods of severely disturbed moods. I suspected Lindsey might also be suffering as a consequence of her husband's depression, and since I knew his chances of recovery were far better if their relationship was stable and supportive, I asked to see her.

Sure enough, she was in trouble. She complained that her life felt like a "vacuum" because of her husband's moodiness, insensitivity, and extended periods of withdrawal. He was like a "deaf-mute," she told me. "He's totally oblivious to my needs, no matter what I do."

It made no difference how vehemently Lindsey would demand Adam's attention. She once tossed the entire contents of his bedroom closet out the window as an act of protest against his sexual disinterest, but he simply had their housekeeper take every garment to the cleaners, never even acknowledging her rage. From Adam's perspective, this incident was just another example of how "emotional and irrational" Lindsey could be. "Maybe her period was coming on, you know, the premenstrual problem," was his explanation to me when I asked him what he had made of the clothes toss.

When I asked Lindsey if she had ever considered leaving Adam, she said she had, but that life as a single woman frightened her. She had seen how hard things were for her divorced friends, and the AIDS-conscious dating scene scared her.

When I quizzed her further, I found that more than just romantic concerns were on Lindsey's mind, however. She had virtually no career skills, and more and more she had been finding it difficult to relate closely with friends. Their only daughter had just left for her first year of college, so Lindsey was feeling more dependent on Adam than ever.

Lindsey's "vacuum" was even emptier than I had thought. She had allowed herself to be totally drained by her husband's condition. For sixteen years, she had focused on her husband rather than on herself, and she had lost herself in the process. No wonder she was looking so angrily to her husband for comfort and support. From her perspective, he had robbed her and now he owed her! And he wasn't delivering.

And yet the sad truth was that the more Lindsey demanded from Adam, the less he was able to give. She was paralyzing him with her needs even more than his depression had him feeling paralyzed already. It was a classic case of fusion making a bad situation worse.

So what was my solution?

First, I needed to treat Adam's depression with antidepressant medication so that his biological symptoms could improve and he could find the energy to deal more effectively with his life. The medication would also help him concentrate well enough to benefit from the psychotherapy I was giving him. He had a great many distorted and negative thoughts that I had to make clear to him. These thoughts were very instrumental in promoting his depressed moods.

While treating Adam, I also started treating Lindsey. My goal was to teach her to defuse, but also to come to grips with the underlying issues that were causing her to fuse in the first place. She was going to have to stop focusing on how depressing it was to live with someone as "emotionally comatose" as her husband and begin facing *why* she found her life with him so depressing.

As it turned out, she felt grossly unprepared to take care of herself financially. This scared her, given the prospect that her relationship with Adam might have to end. She also was suffering from the recent departure of her daughter to college. It left a huge void, which Adam, in his depressed state, was woefully unable to fill. The result was Lindsey's "anger," which actually was being motivated by her own fear. She feared she would have to feel inadequate and alone for the rest of her life.

I urged Lindsey to concentrate on embellishing her own life rather than focusing on how deficient her husband was. She should expect emotional support from Adam—and I promised her this support would be coming as his condition improved—but taking charge of the emptiness in her own life would have to be her first concern.

I then asked them to start seeing me together rather than individually, and we started to work on getting the fine points of defusing down more clearly. Adam needed to understand that his depression and withdrawal threatened Lindsey. She felt insecure and inadequate anyway, so to see her husband fading as a source of support was a very frightening, dangerous experience for her. Her way of showing her fear, however, was to become angry—angry at Adam for making her feel the fear that she did. She held him responsible for the emotional desolation she felt was overtaking her life.

Adam expressed surprise at this at first, as I suspected he would. His obliviousness to conditions around him, after all, was a symptom of his depression. He would have to start taking responsibility for this lack of awareness, however, if he wanted his relationship with Lindsey to last. We weren't going to ask him to become a social fireball overnight, but he was going to have to begin at least poking his head out of his shell. He had to realize that his self-centered and self-protective reactions to his depressed moods had turned him into an emotional mummy. It was time to unwrap.

Yes, Adam suffered from a serious depressive disorder, but no longer was it an excuse to be insensitive to those around him, and especially to his wife who so desperately needed his support. Becoming aware of Lindsey's needs would actually be therapeutic for his depression, I told him. He was suffering from feelings of inadequacy and isolation just like she was, so by helping to lift her, he'd also be lifting himself.

And how did Lindsey and Adam respond to my advice?

Slowly but surely. Lindsey became more capable of accepting Adam's emotional limitations, knowing that he was working hard to correct them. She also began demanding less of him thanks to her part-time job as a fund-raiser for the American Cancer Society, exercise class, and two nights of bridge a week. Adam also started doing much better as he became reawakened to the pleasures of giving more to Lindsey than just his paycheck.

Step Six: Being Honest with Yourself

Lindsey learned something very important in the months it took her to reevaluate her relationship with Adam. She learned that you cannot conquer what you cannot face. If guilt or fear is the primary force behind the way you are currently interacting with your depressed loved one, you need to admit it.

I'm not saying you need to admit it to your loved one, but you do need to admit it to yourself. How can you expect to come to any kind of understanding of what's going on inside your loved one, after all, until you know what's going on inside of you? And how can you expect to bring any kind of calm to your relationship as long as your own internal conflicts keep raging? Confronting your truest feelings is a crucial aspect of the defusion process. As the quotation from Thomas à Kempis at the beginning of this chapter points out, you can't bring peace to anyone else until you've brought peace to yourself.

But you *are* being honest, you say? That's why you insist on letting your loved one know how upset he makes you feel?

As we found with Lindsey, there's a difference between expressing *how* you feel and expressing *why* you feel. Lindsey was all too willing to let Adam know that his emotional insensitivity made her feel neglected and angry, but she was much *less* willing to acknowledge what *really* made her feel this way. This is typical of the fusion process.

You blame *how* you feel on the actions of your loved one, but you do not take the next step and ask yourself what is going on *inside you* that causes you to react the way you do. You allow your moods to be dictated by your partner's moods—and a resentment builds that inevitably gives birth to the fusion process. You feel like an emotional slave to your loved one and it angers you, yet the bondage is one that *you* do much to create.

Precisely because you *have* created this bondage, however, you are in the best position to break it. That's the attitude you must adopt if you're going to be successful in stopping the destructive emotional struggles you and your loved one are having. You're the one who's gotten yourself into this mess, so you're the best one to get yourself out.

Yes, professional treatment is ready to give you a helping hand, as we'll see in Chapter 6. But the most important work will have to be done by you. More than any psychotherapist or antidepressant drug, you have the power to stop the fusion that's ruining your relationship and your life.

Step Seven: Finding the Right Emotional Distance

The six defusion strategies we've seen so far all have had the common goal of reducing the emotional friction between you and your loved one, because it's this friction that produces the sparks that keep fusion aflame. This is especially true of our seventh and final strategy, which I call finding the right emotional distance. It's a critical aspect of the defusion process and yet often a very difficult one, because it hits at the very heart of why a relationship becomes fused in the first place.

In Chapter 3 I told you that fusion has a way of blurring the boundaries between you and your loved one. It literally begins to destroy your individuality, so that you start to lose sight of whose problems really belong to whom. You begin to believe that curing your loved one's problems is the key to curing your own problems, and he begins to believe that your meddlesome ways are causing his problems in the first place. This creates the confusion that keeps fusion alive.

The first six strategies of my program can do a great deal to minimize this confusion, as we've seen, but it's going to be important to find the right distance from which to implement them, a distance that allows you to show your partner that you still care, but that you're also going to be looking out for yourself.

"But wait a minute," you may be thinking. "Isn't greater intimacy the goal of this book? Why should I be pulling away from my partner when my ultimate wish is to grow closer?"

I understand that concern and respect it greatly, but I also must tell you something quite basic about human relationships: You can't expect to build a strong house on a weak foundation. Depending on the amount of damage your relationship has suffered, it's going to be crucial to get each of you stable before we put you back together. You'll only be destabilized by fusion if we do not. This means that you're going to have to get to the point where you feel well adjusted and secure, and it also means that your loved one's depression will have to be resolved. You can't expect to reconstruct a relationship of any lasting worth until both occur.

What sort of distance am I talking about, and how do you achieve it?

Don't worry; it's not something that requires any sort of formal bilateral agreement. You simply work toward a level of interaction with your loved one that walks the line between roof-raising arguments and stony silence. If you're at each other's throats with every spoken word, then you're fusing, and the distance between you is too small. If you're not speaking at all, fusion also is at work, and the distance between you is too great. Your goal should be to find some reasonably peaceful territory in between, territory where you'll probably still feel disappointment that things aren't going better, but where you'll at least be thankful that the wars of fusion are finally gone.

Staying in this territory might not be easy at times. You may begin to feel guilty for not being more involved with your loved one's depression. Or, the detachment could make you begin to face certain uncomfortable truths about yourself or your relationship. You may even begin to *miss* the heated exchanges or cat-and-mouse games you used to have with your loved one, but you mustn't slip back into being fused.

Establishing this proper emotional distance can do more than just allow each of you to heal. It can begin to carve out new patterns of communication that could be the beginnings of a new and more realistic order. When two people become fused, it's usually because one person feels abandoned while the other feels smothered. This mismatch creates the conflict that keeps fusion aglow.

I mention this because, although we all have ideal levels of intimacy that we would *like* to be able to share with our loved ones, it's important not to let these ideal levels get in the way of the levels we *realistically* can expect. The person you're living with simply may not be capable of satisfying your intimacy needs, and especially not if he or she is depressed. You're going to have to be patient, and you may have to be willing to compromise if you want your relationship to survive. As we'll be seeing later in this book, the person who demands the most intimacy may not really even be able to handle it if and when it comes. It's easy to clamor for something, after all, when you know it's not going to be coming. It's even possible that you *both* may be fearful of truly close emotional communication, though one of you complains about getting far too little.

I understand it may go against your emotional inclinations, but disengaging to an emotional distance that avoids fusion must be your goal if you're hoping for greater closeness with your depressed loved one at some future date. It may feel like a move in the wrong direction at first, but trust me when I say it's the only way to go if you have any hope for a healthy future. Rick and Lynn's relationship makes this point very well.

Rick and Lynn had been married for twelve years, and although Lynn had always been somewhat reserved and withdrawn, she became decidedly worse following the death of her mother. Rick was able to deal with the change for a while, but eventually he began to resent his wife's coldness and withdrawal and the two became fused in argumentative struggles that were psychologically very damaging for both of them.

"She just won't let me get close to her. We're lucky to have sex twice a month, and when we do it's almost not worth it. She's just passionless, so preoccupied and self-absorbed. She says she still loves me, but if this is love, I'm not sure I want it."

Rick's first reaction to feeling rejected by Lynn was to do some sulking of his own, but when that didn't accomplish anything he started getting more aggressive. He'd snap at her for things she wasn't doing around the house and accuse her of being a crybaby. This caused Lynn to withdraw even more, which frustrated Rick even further. They became hopelessly fused.

I told Rick that his wife was probably in need of professional treatment, but that just as important, he was going to have to give her some emotional breathing room if the treatment was going to work. This breathing room would allow him to pull himself together too, I told him, because by backing off he'd be putting a stop to the rejection that was damaging his ego—and hence making him need his wife's support even more. He had gotten himself into a situation where his attempts at a solution were only aggravating his problem—a very common "catch-22" of the fusion process.

Lynn was probably never going to be the emotional cuddly toy of his dreams, but he was going to have to accept that. He was going to have to understand that his wife had emotional needs different from his own and that her depression was making those differences even more pronounced. He also was going to have to realize that by expressing anger and disappointment he was only distancing his wife even more.

At first, Rick had feelings of guilt about disengaging from Lynn's problem, and also some fear about having to learn to be more independent. But I convinced him that only by disengaging and focusing on strengthening himself could he expect their relationship to improve.

Rick took my advice. He started talking less to Lynn about their problems, spending more time in activities with friends, and reestablishing a higher level of interest at work. This not only gave him an added confidence that he came to realize he had needed all along, but it helped Lynn get back on her feet. When Rick gave her the space she needed, she was better able to come to grips with her condition. She also stopped resenting Rick for being so demanding and was able to be more giving as a result. It was another case where minor concessions led to major gains via the establishment of a proper emotional distance.

INDEPENDENCE IS THE BEST MEDICINE

As we saw with Rick, and Lindsey before that, deep involvement with your loved one's problems could be a sign that you're attempting to escape problems of your own. You also could be revealing fears you have about your own level of dependency: You may fear that you will not be able to live a fulfilling life unless your partner gets well enough to give you the love and support you feel you need.

If that's true, you must get to work on putting those fears

behind you. You must have the courage to acknowledge whatever shortcomings, *from your side of the fence,* could be contributing to your relationship problems and get to work on correcting them. Not until you accept this responsibility will your situation have a chance to improve.

Accepting this responsibility may not be easy at first. It may require that you undergo psychiatric counseling, as we'll be seeing in Chapter 6. But whether that becomes necessary or not, you must be willing to shift the way you're currently thinking. You must realize that you can be happy and successful, whether your loved one gets well or not. The sooner you begin thinking this way, the better off you will be—and the better off your partner will be, because you'll no longer be draining his or her energy (which may be at rock bottom already). Your loved one has his hands full with his own troubles—he doesn't need the additional burden of shouldering yours.

The bottom line is that the better you can feel about yourself, the better you'll be able to function as a supportive and healing force. You may have to make some major changes in your current life-style to become this healing force, but it will be well worth it for all concerned. You're going to have to find ways to reinvest the negative energy that you're presently expending in the fusion process, and believe me—that energy is considerable. One roof-raising ballyhoo, or several sleepless nights, and, as you may have noticed, you're limp.

So stop wasting that energy! Start putting it to new, productive, and *enjoyable* use. The more you can improve yourself, the more you'll be improving your situation. Your loved one may find fault with your efforts at greater independence at first, but if you hang tough, he'll eventually get the message that you mean business. He'll see that his partner in depression is getting well, and that if he's going to stay miserable, he's going to have to do it alone.

What sort of independence efforts am I talking about?

Anything that builds self-esteem and independence.

I've had patients take up exercise, the arts, additional education, careers, second careers, charitable efforts, and entrepreneurial efforts. Anything that can help you rekindle your zest for life—in addition to simply removing you from excessive involvement with your depressed partner—is going to help your situation. You're going to feel less trapped, less dependent, less empty, and less a victim of your loved one's condition. This, in turn, is going to make you feel less resentful and angry and hence less prone to engage in fusion skirmishes. Remember: The happier you can become, the happier your loved one will be forced to become, because he'll no longer have your misery to feed from. Just as depression is contagious, so is joy.

But more on that in Chapter 8. Let's take a look now at the kind of outside pursuits that can give you the strength to break free, and remain free, of fusion.

CAREER EFFORTS

If you're not currently employed, I strongly suggest you begin looking into a career of some type. Work contributes to independence by giving you income, positive feedback, and a feeling of productivity. This isn't to say you should grab the nearest job at the local supermarket, but even that might not be such a bad idea if it would get you into a more positive environment. There's nothing wrong with boosting your ego with a paycheck, regardless of where the decimal point may fall. Your first goal should be to get your mind off your depressed partner. And don't feel you have to accomplish anything spectacular. Start with small steps and the leaps will come.

If a job would only depress you further, however, then let your pleasure be your guide. Pursue something that's been a lifelong interest, something that will stimulate you, challenge you, and help you grow. One of my patients has become an outstanding artist, while another is currently working toward a Ph.D. in psychology with the hope of counseling people on many of the same problems addressed in this book. She tells me that she's finally feeling fulfilled after so many years of feeling drained, and that many of her husband's behaviors that used to provoke her now just run right off her back. She's feeling good enough about herself and her future that she no longer finds her husband's depression such a threat.

COMMUNITY SERVICE

Volunteer work also can be a great ego booster, even better than gainful employment if your finances are not a concern. You'll feel you're doing something positive and kind, which will be a welcome change from the negative and hurtful energy you've been expending in your fused struggles with your loved one. Charitable efforts also can help you get a different perspective on your troubles, as seeing what it means to be truly sick or needy can help you see your own problems in a less dismal light.

"I was about to unload on my husand for leaving his underwear on the floor the other night, but it suddenly seemed so trivial," one patient told me after her first week of working with cancer patients at a large municipal hospital. "I'm finding it takes a lot more to upset me now. I feel like I'm doing something really important, and it's made me a different person."

FRIENDSHIPS

For intellectual stimulation, the latest gossip, a good laugh or a good cry—there's nothing like a good friend. And yet it is characteristic for fused couples to push their friendships aside. They lose contact with friends because they focus so intently on themselves. This leads to emotional isolation, which fuels their fusion even more.

That's why it's so important to bring friends back into your life. Don't bring them back just to rehash the horrors you're going through with your depressed partner, however, because you're trying to free yourself from those thoughts. Nor do you want to bring your friends into the fusion you're experiencing with your loved one. Do things with your friends that you have *not* been able to do with your loved one. And don't be deterred by complaints that your partner may raise. Yes, he might complain of feeling abandoned, but he may need to feel some discomfort if he's going to get the message that he needs help. And you cannot be of help unless you are feeling strong and independent.

HEALTH PURSUITS

I could write a book about this topic alone. When people become fused, they tend to reach in all the wrong places for ways to soothe their pain: alcohol, drugs, compulsive overeating, gambling—the list is a decidedly unhealthy one. These behaviors can provide relief temporarily, of course, but they only create pains of their own in the long run. They also demonstrate a relinquishing of control when what's so desperately needed by victims of fusion is gaining control. Victims of fusion need to feel that they can make a difference in how they feel and in what happens to their lives.

That's why health pursuits—good diet and sensible exercise habits—can be great metaphors as well as effective biological remedies for many types of depression caused by the fusion process. Good exercise habits can help fight depression and anxiety by stirring up mood-elevating brain chemicals called endorphins. Exercise can also create feelings of self-confidence by improving physical appearance and stamina. I'm not saying diet and exercise can be miracle cures, but I am saying that physically, as well as symbolically, behaviors that improve the body are part of taking care of the psyche.

SUPPORT GROUPS

Yes, your goal should be to get your mind *off* your fusion-provoking loved one, but sometimes that's not possible until certain underlying angers have been vented and important issues have been addressed. And that's where support groups and/or professional counseling can help.

Groups such as AA, NA (Narcotics Anonymous), Alanon, Rational Recovery, Adult Children of Alcoholics, Emotions Anonymous, Codependency Groups, Overeaters Anonymous, and the Manic Depressive and Depressive associations are just a few of the organizations now available to help you. Most of the members of these groups also will have experienced significant fusion with loved ones of their own, so you'll be assured of being able to compare notes. Even more important, however, you'll be able to voice your deepest feelings and frustrations without having to vent these feelings on your loved one and hence add further to the fusion that's destroying your life.

What Successful Self-Management Can Give You

You've reached the end of the first part of my three-part plan for defusing fusion, and I hope you've learned that, as much as your loved one, you too, play a role in the fusion process. Until you've learned to be less flammable, the fires will continue to burn.

But by learning to understand and manage your anger, recognizing and avoiding fusion "sparks," maintaining a safe, stable emotional distance from your partner that minimizes fusion-provoking exchanges, and working toward a more rewarding life of your own, you can tailor yourself a flameproof suit. What you can expect by wearing this suit, moreover, is considerable:

▲ Relief from the fighting, hostility, and tension, whether your loved one gets well or not.
▲ The establishment of an environment ideal for maximizing the chances that your loved one will get well.
▲ A chance to regain control of your own life in a way that

is no longer vulnerable to the destructive forces of your partner's depressed state.

Put quite simply, when fusion is the problem, defusion is the solution. It would be nice if your loved one could stop provoking you in the first place, but until he or she has undergone a considerable period of professional treatment, that's not likely to happen. This means that the responsibility for creating a defused environment rests with you. Your loved one may continue to throw matches, but you're going to have to stop becoming inflamed. Keep in mind, too, that by creating a defused environment, you deprive your loved one of the turmoil he or she has been using as camouflage for his condition. If the fires stop burning and there's no more smoke, your loved one will have a better chance of seeing his disturbed state for what it is.

That being said, let's look now at the other side of the fusion equation: the depressed behavior of your loved one, which has been causing all the sparks to fly in the first place.

How to Defuse, Step Two:
Managing Your Loved One

"In adversity, keep an even mind."

HORACE, 65–8 B.C.

"I wish you could have been there, Doctor. He turned absolutely purple and started chewing me out right there in front of our neighbor. The woman is 70 years old, and there's my husband laying into me with every four-letter word in the book. How do you stay defused in a situation like that?"

Jennifer, a slim, attractive 38-year-old sales rep, was recounting a fracas in which her husband, Dean, a 42-year-old banker, had accused her of intentionally backing over his new ten-speed bike, which he had parked in the driveway. Her question was a good one. How *do* you deal with your partner during the all-important defusion process? You can be doing all the right things to manage yourself to stay defused, but who's going to tend to your unmanageable loved one?

Sorry, but that's your job, too. Professional treatment will have a calming effect on your partner—if he or she agrees to receive it—but *how you deal with your partner* is going to have a powerful impact on how effective that treatment will be. There also are apt to be relapses in your partner's recovery, so you're going to have to learn to manage those as well. Depression is not like a cold or flu that just clears up overnight: Even when successfully treated, it can recur.

"So what am I supposed to do—shoot my husband with a stun gun when he goes wild like that?" Jennifer asked.

"In a manner of speaking, yes," I told her.

What we're going to see in this chapter is that you, as much as any psychotherapist or medication therapy, have the power to help your partner in ways that are crucial for him to get well. This may shock you, but you must remember what we've learned about the contagious nature of depressive disorders. If you allow your loved one to continue to behave in his "sick" manner when he's in your presence, his condition will not only worsen, but make you feel worse, as well.

This is why the self-management strategies we discussed in Chapter 4 are not going to be enough if you really want to maximize your chances of eliminating the toxic and contagious effects of your partner's depression once and for all. Yes, you can protect yourself to a degree, purely by learning to manage yourself. But by neglecting to manage your partner, you allow his depressive "germs" to continue to fill the air. This puts you at the constant risk of becoming reinfected and then passing *your* depressed or agitated behavior back to your partner.

React for the Future, Not the Present

When I told that to Jennifer, she seemed to know precisely what I was talking about. As hard as she would try to insulate herself from her husband's horrid moods, they would anger her, and the anger would build. Finally she would "lose it," as she lost it in the driveway that day, and fusion would break out.

"I could handle the swearing, but it was when he started accusing me of destroying his bike on purpose that I cracked. He tried to tell me that I felt threatened when he exercised, that I didn't want him to get in shape, because it might mean losing him to another woman. But I'm the one who bought him the damned bike in the first place. I thought it would help get him out of his depressed periods when he does nothing but sit in front of the television and sleeps ten hours a day."

"So how did you respond to his accusations?" I asked.

"I told him that if attracting other women was his goal, he'd have to ride from here to Mars and back again to have a chance. I know it was the wrong thing to do, but it sure made me feel better at the time."

Jennifer had made a classic mistake. She had allowed herself to react in a way that made her feel better for the moment, but which would make her feel a whole lot worse in the future. Dean retreated in a huff following the incident in the driveway and didn't speak to her for three days. Jennifer felt angry, powerless, and rejected. They had only increased the level of fusion between them.

"So what should I have done? Just sit there and take that kind of insane abuse?" she asked.

There are a number of things Jennifer could have done, all of which would have achieved the important goal of avoiding a fusion eruption while also preserving her dignity. This is crucial to keep in mind as you read through these partner-management strategies. Yes, you want to avoid fusion, but not simply by running away from it. You must make it clear to your partner *why* you're choosing to avoid another fusion skirmish, and you must appear highly rational and in control when you do so. The following confrontational techniques can help you.

Shift the Focus from "You to "I"

One of the best ways of achieving a dignified exit from a potential fusion flare-up is simply to shift the focus. If you can remember to say "I" where you might otherwise have said "you," you'll find a huge difference in the impact of your words. For example, Jennifer might have handled her enraged husband in this way:

"I can see that I've upset you, and I'm sorry. But it must be obvious that I didn't mean to destroy your bike, because I've damaged my car in the process. I may have been careless, but I don't deserve to be humiliated. I'm becoming very upset by our argument and won't discuss it further until we can *both* calm down."

Notice the shift—everything goes into the first person. Even when Jennifer could have said "I'm becoming upset by *your* behavior," she says she's being upset by "our argument." What this shift does is remove the accusatory tone that "you" implies. Even though Jennifer might feel that her husband is to blame for the altercation they're having, it does more harm than good to announce that opinion when her husband is in such a volatile state. Jennifer stands a much better chance of getting her point across later when each of them has calmed down, which is why she says she will not discuss the matter any further until they both are calm. This leaves each of them with the personal responsibility for getting calm. Without mutual calming, her reasoning and explaining stands only to get engulfed in more fusion.

Let me give you another example of how this "you" to "I" shift can greatly reduce the likelihood of fusion flare-ups when altercations arise. Alan and Robin have been married for ten years, but few of them have been easy ones because Alan has had to change jobs six times. The job changes have upset Robin greatly, so it's with considerable trepidation that she begins to hear Alan talk of yet another potential move one night after he returns home from work. Alan also has experienced episodes of fairly serious depression throughout their marriage—episodes usually associated with his job changes—so Robin has reason to be doubly concerned when he comes home expressing thoughts of yet another career shift. How should she react?

In the past, Robin would have accused Alan of being irresponsible, unfocused, and concerned about himself—which would have caused him to accuse her of being an uncaring, domineering bitch. But this time she tries a different tack.

"I'm sorry to hear that things aren't going well, Alan, and I want to listen to you, but the thought of having to pull up our roots again just when I've finally settled into a community I like upsets me very much. I just don't think I can cope with another move, so if that's going to be the topic of our discussion, I'm not going to be able to continue given the way I feel. But if we can talk about the problems that you're having at work, and how we might work together to solve them, then I'm willing to talk and help you in any way I can."

Robin's willingness to acknowledge her own limitations, along with her heartfelt interest in helping Alan get to the bottom of his latest career dilemma, was a major shift from the way she used to attack him in the past. This made a very strong impression on Alan because he felt supported for a change instead of disparaged. The two went on to have a very productive discussion about how he might confront rather than run away from his latest career problem.

MAKE SELF-PROTECTION "JOB #1"

If you look closely at the examples of Jennifer and Robin, you'll see how each was able to determine when she was approaching her limit in terms of how much negative emotional arousal she could absorb before losing her ability to remain objective and calm. This is something you absolutely *must* learn to do if you're going to have any chance of keeping a therapeutic peace between you and your depressed partner.

You must learn to protect yourself *from* your partner if you're going to be of any help *to* your partner. That might sound strange, but let's not forget what we know about the fusion process. The more you allow yourself to be upset, the more you behave in ways that upset your partner, and wham:

You've got anger begetting anger in the uncontrollable emotional chain reaction that this book is all about.

So repeat it again: "By protecting myself, I protect my loved one." I can't emphasize enough how important this self-protection policy is going to be in putting a stop to the fusion between you. As uncaring as it may seem, you must keep your partner at a distance that allows you to feel safe, because only by feeling safe will you be able to stay defused and help your partner confront his problem productively. The tension, fear, and frustration in your relationship must be allowed to lift. Neither you nor your loved one will be able to heal if they do not.

THE ART AND SCIENCE OF SETTING LIMITS

I feel so strongly about the importance of establishing limits to how much harassment you will endure from your partner that I recommend you actually commit some limit-setting remarks to memory. Don't feel you need to remember them word for word, but do remember their gist. They can come in very handy when the heat of the moment has you groping for the right words only to come up with the wrong ones.

And remember: You're putting the focus on *your limitations in being able to cope* rather than on the behavior of your partner that is forcing you to cope in the first place. This doesn't mean you should accept the blame in an altercation, because blame shouldn't even be an issue. Your goal should simply be to announce that the argument is producing levels of hostility and anger that you're finding upsetting to a point of being counterproductive to meaningful discussion.

▲ "I can see that you're upset, but I won't be able to remain calm enough to listen if you continue talking with that much anger."

▲ "I may have been wrong and I may have been insensitive to your needs, but I don't deserve to be subjected to this level of abuse. I'd prefer to talk after we've each had a chance to calm down."

▲ "I know that your silence means you're hurt and upset, but I'm reacting to your silence with such tension that I'm finding it difficult to cope. Please let me know when you're ready to talk."

▲ "Please stop, I'm starting to feel frightened. I'm sure you have good reason to be upset, but I'm having difficulty with the fear I'm feeling right now, so I'm going to leave the room. Please let me know when we can talk without so much anger."

▲ "I know you're feeling down, and I understand that you need to talk it out, but I just can't absorb any more pain and sadness right now. Let's stop for a while and talk more later when I'm in a mood that can be of more help."

Notice the shift? And notice the tone? There's no blaming, but rather only stating of fact, and while you're being *compassionate* you're also being *firm*. Your partner may well accuse you of being lily-livered for refusing to go tooth and nail, but stick to your guns. You're not surrendering, but instead are changing the rules of battle. No fury allowed—and hence no fusion. Each of you will stand to be the winner if you can learn to "fight" in this more civil way.

AVOID THE "KINDLING POINT"

When I talk to my patients about the importance of protecting themselves from the emotional arrows being shot by their partners, I frequently use the analogy of what's known in physics as the "kindling point." It's that critical temperature at which something teeters between going out or going up in flames—and if you're fused with your loved one, you'll see why the analogy applies. Your partner drops a "spark," to which you respond with emotional heat of your own, and before you know it the house is afire. Or maybe you drop the spark and your partner responds, but either way you've got a major blaze on your hands.

What this means is that you've got to stop that critical kindling point from being reached. Your disturbed partner is going to continue to provoke you for as along as he or she remains depressed, and you're going to have to accept that. You may also slip from time to time and drop a few sparks of your own, but this doesn't mean that major fires have to break out. If you can learn to sense when that critical "kindling point" is being approached, you can prevent the raging conflagrations that have been consuming your relationship.

This is why protecting yourself by setting limits with your partner is so important. You must not allow your loved one to generate the kind of emotional heat capable of setting you ablaze. You must know when to lower the temperature by pulling away.

But couldn't a good, firm "Shut up, you screwball!" do the same thing, especially when your loved one is being so outrageous?

Don't we both wish it could. Confrontations like that only exacerbate the problem. You must learn the fine art of getting by giving. By making what may appear to be concessions in head-to-head confrontations, you will gain far more than you'll lose, and the gains will be for your loved one as well as for you. Try to keep that in mind when you think you may be swallowing your pride by employing my peacekeeping strategies. The trauma-free environment you're working to create is the environment each of you needs if you're going to be able to put your current troubles behind you. Research leaves little doubt that the ability to think rationally drops off sharply as levels of anger rise, so if any real progress is going to be made in your confrontations, cool heads are going to have to prevail.

Rules for Fighting Right

I'd like to get more specific about the confrontational techniques you'll need to keep you and your loved one's emotions from reaching destructive levels. Let's imagine that you've successfully avoided a fusion flare-up by using one of my limit-setting phrases presented earlier, but now it's time to discuss the issue further after each of you has calmed down. What should you expect, and how should you proceed?

First of all, let me warn you that, as in a boxing match with a formidable challenger, you may have to go more than just one round before arriving at a resolution, especially if the two of you are evenly matched—which, if you've been fused, I'm going to guess you are. You may find yourselves slugging it out especially hard in the early rounds, as the same negative arousal will be generated that made you postpone your confrontation in the first place. Be patient, and don't be afraid to call for more time out if things get too hot. Just come back each time more committed than ever to keeping things cool enough to be constructive. The following confrontational techniques can help you.

FOCUS ON FEELINGS, NOT ACTIONS OR WORDS

If you and your loved one are fused, I can guarantee that you've been fighting about actions and words rather than the feelings behind those actions and words. One of you says or does something the other disapproves of, and an attack ensues that focuses on that only. How each of you actually *feels* about the act or comment gets lost somewhere in the ruckus. Consider the recent altercation between two patients of mine, Jerry and Adele.

Jerry and Adele have been married for twenty-five years, most of which have seen Jerry go in and out of some fairly serious depressive episodes. Jerry had been doing well, but he slipped back into a down period in which he began neglecting Adele emotionally as well as sexually. Adele responded to this relapse, unfortunately, with accusations that Jerry was an uncaring and basically selfish wretch who was incapable of love and affection. Never once did she mention how she actually *felt* about his withdrawal, however. Here's how she might have handled the situation more wisely:

"I'm sorry I became so upset last night, Jerry, but you know that when you withdraw from me I begin to doubt myself. I know I have insecurities of my own that make me feel this way, but I can't help that, just as you may not be able to help yourself from feeling depressed. I also understand that lots of times you're not even aware that you're depressed or that you are withdrawing. If you think we can work through this by ourselves, I'm willing to help in any way I can, but unless things get better I think we should get you back to your doctor. I'll certainly go with you to any joint sessions that might be necessary."

Notice the shift away from Jerry's *actions* to how Adele actually *felt* about those actions. This technique is important because it cuts through to the real issue at stake when you argue. Your loved one's behavior is not what's bothering you— it's how his behavior has made you feel. As a result, your feelings are what need to be discussed. If you get caught up in arguing over your loved one's actions, you'll never get to what really matters. Even if Jerry denies that he is withdrawing, he can't deny that Adele has feelings about his withdrawal, and that she has a right to discuss them. This puts a legitimate pressure on Jerry to address the issue, which he might otherwise dismiss as merely a hurtful accusation from a wife who is "out for blood."

EMPATHIZE BEFORE YOU CRITICIZE

Notice, too, how Adele expressed some understanding and even acceptance of Jerry's problem. She even went the next step and admitted to having emotional weaknesses of her own. This accomplished something very important: It allowed Jerry to feel he had an ally rather than an enemy in dealing with his problems and maximized his receptivity to the idea that he might need professional help. Had Adele continued to disparage Jerry for his depressed behavior, she'd have encouraged him to defend that behavior or, worse yet, to deny it. This would have moved Jerry in precisely the opposite direction he needs to go to get well.

So remember: An ounce of empathy can be worth a pound of aspersion when it comes to helping your loved one out of his depressed state. When your partner falls victim to one of his depressed moods, learn to see him as just that—a victim. Yes, you also are going to be a victim as his or her behavior begins to affect you, but that's precisely the scenario you and your partner must learn to see. *Both of you are victims together,* and you're not victims of each other, but rather of the fusion being generated by your loved one's emotionally impaired state. Once you realize this, you can stop attacking each other and begin attacking the real villain that's destroying your relationship.

Consider "Fault" A Dirty Word

I hear it so often from patients when they complain of how their depressed partners are ruining their lives. "If I didn't have this person dragging me down, I'd be happy, successful, and free."

But would you be saying this if your loved one had a serious physical impairment like heart disease or cancer?

Probably not. You'd be afraid, and even though you'd be upset that an illness was threatening your lives, you'd be feeling sympathy and be doing everything possible to help fight the illness and lend support.

"But people with heart disease don't accuse you of things that are hurtful and totally untrue," Jennifer said to me, referring to the incident in the driveway with Dean.

"But now that you understand the symptoms of depression, can't you see that faulting Dean for his actions that day was like faulting a heart-disease patient for having an attack of angina?" was my answer.

My point is simply this: There must be no element of blame in any of the confrontations you and your loved one have. There must only be the *acceptance of the reality that your loved one is suffering from a diagnosable mood disturbance,* which—through cooperation from each of you—can be treated and improved. If any "fault" exists, it will only be in *your* failure to acknowledge this and respond accordingly.

Never Assume You Know Intent

"But he means to hurt me. You can tell me he doesn't, but I just can't believe it. There's such anger and fear in him that it scares me."

"Sorry, Jennifer, but that anger and fear has much more to do with him than it does with you, and it may have existed long before the two of you ever met."

It can be extremely difficult not to feel that your loved one's hurtful behavior is intended, but to do so only reflects a gross misunderstanding of how depressive illnesses work on the human brain. They "cross the wires," so to speak. They give the depressed person a distorted view of the world, which leads to distorted behavior as a result. Many times what you're seeing from a depressed person are "projections"—assessments of outside situations that, in truth, reflect his own inner opinions of himself. When Dean accused Jennifer of being afraid of losing him to another woman, he was, in fact, expressing his fear of losing her. This fear was likely to have been the motivating factor behind his workouts—and yet Dean did not know it. His depression was preventing him from truly understanding his own motivations.

So please—do yourself and your depressed partner the favor of not assuming you know his intentions. His intentions may not be clear even to him. Thinking that you know his purpose, moreover, will imply a kind of supremacy on your part that I can guarantee will heighten the pain of your altercations.

But your partner is hurting you whether he means to or not, and you think that on some level—subconscious though it may be—he does mean to cause you pain.

You could be right, because insecurity and hidden hostilities often can take aggressive forms, but this doesn't change the fact that it makes no sense for you to react emotionally to these aggressions from your loved one. You must learn to accept the realities of your partner's depression and deal with them in the least emotional and most rational ways possible.

When Talking Makes Things Worse—Learning How to Move In and Move Out

This rule for productive conversations with your loved one requires you to know which issues promote fusion so much that they just cannot be discussed at length. That may sound strange or "anticommunicational," but it's true when your relationship is plagued by fusion.

You must use tact and strategy when talking about certain issues and be sensitive to what I referred to earlier as the "kindling point" if you're going to avoid fusion eruptions. You can do this by moving in and moving out of conversations—stating your feelings calmly and objectively and in a way that does not pass judgment on your partner—and them moving out before fusion can begin. This maintains your own sense of emotional safety while it lets your partner know where you stand—all without being overly provocative. You make your points when you move in and move out, but you don't stick around to defend them.

Consider the case of Tom and Marsha, for example, whom we met in Chapter 1. The two would have a ballyhoo every time Marsha would approach Tom about his drinking. The conversation would always proceed the same way, with Tom challenging Marsha to recall exactly *when* he had consumed too much. Then the two would begin arguing over the *exact* drink count. This would lead to multiple insults, accusations, recollections of past hurts, and blaming by each of them. The conversations always followed the same path, and always ended in chaos.

I advised Marsha to handle Tom's drinking differently. I told her to respond to an increase in his consumption by expressing concern that he might be feeling depressed. If Tom retorted with his usual defensiveness and fervor, she should simply move out of the conversation by saying, "You know how scared I get when I think your depression is returning, so I just wanted to tell you what I was observing. I'm not going to get into it anymore than that, because I realize that I've got to manage my own fears. In the meantime, please just start to pay attention and see if you think you might be having some problems that need help."

Notice that Marsha refused to fuse, respected the volatility of the topic, and took responsibility for her end of the conversation. She moved in, made a constructive observation, and moved out. She was careful to avoid accusation and would not allow their usual script to play out.

Use Humor Whenever Possible

"I'll never forget how good it felt," Jennifer told me. And no, she wasn't talking about sex. She was talking about the first laugh she and Dean had been able to share in over six months.

When I started seeing Jennifer, she and Dean were as fused as two people can be. If they talked at all, they would argue, and usually quite heatedly. The row in the driveway had been just one of many such incidents that had become common in their relationship. Each felt constantly on guard against being attacked by the other, so even minor offenses would be interpreted as major crimes. A tension had developed between them that was making any communication other than outright insults impossible.

"So why not do something to break all that tension?" I suggested to Jennifer one day. "If you can do something to get a laugh or even a smile out of Dean, I think you'll see an amazing release of the tension that's built up between you. Your quarrels are only adding to that tension, because they're further convincing each of you that the other is being disapproving and hateful. If you can do something that shows, in a humorous way, that you're willing to try to see things from Dean's point of view, I think you'll see some new and very valuable lines of communication opening up."

Jennifer took my advice marvelously. She decided to make light of a bad habit she had of not paying attention to what she bought at the supermarket. She could wind up accumulating three or four of the same items in the refrigerator without even knowing it. This would annoy Dean as it was needlessly wasteful, which in turn would cause Jennifer to see Dean as hypercritical and petty. More than a few fusion eruptions had been started by one too many half-empty cartons of milk in the fridge.

"So I lined up about eight containers of yogurt on the counter one morning and wrote Dean a note asking him not to forget to stop for yogurt that night on his way home from work," Jennifer told me during a session recently. "It worked. He came home with a smile that night. And even some yogurt. We talked, got some things ironed out, and it turned out to be our first enjoyable evening in a long time."

Humor can assist you in rising above the seeming hopelessness of your situation by helping you establish new and less combative ground rules for communication. Jennifer's little joke had invited Dean to view her in a new and less threatening light. She was not the blindly judgmental bitch he had accused her of being, but rather someone capable of acknowledging her own shortcomings—and hence someone who could be understanding of his.

It was an act of concession, a way of saying that neither of them was perfect—but it was also a warm, playful act between a man and a woman. Jennifer was saying that she was not only comfortable with her own imperfections, but was accepting of Dean's limitations and still desired him. Why destroy each other for failing to live up to the impossible? Yes, Jennifer would try to be better about keeping inventory of the refrigerator, and hopefully Dean would be better at keeping inventory of his problems. The important thing was for Dean to know that Jennifer still very much valued his companionship.

One note of warning about humor, however. Be very careful when making your partner the subject of your levity. Sarcasm can wind the vise of fusion even tighter. If you want there to be a benefactor of your jokes, it's best to keep yourself as their butt.

Don't Fight About Sex (or with It, Either)

Patients often will confess to accusing their depressed partners of sexual inadequacy when heated arguments arise, and I must tell you that it's a very cheap shot to take. Diminished sex drive can be caused by depression for physiological as well as psychological reasons. Your insensitivity to this reality is apt to make your partner's inadequacy only worse, moreover, so you lose in two respects.

But your partner is withholding sex to punish you, you say, so why be nice?

I agree that it's possible that your partner is withholding sex out of anger and hurt promoted by the fusion in your relationship, but that only adds more weight to my advice. You're not likely to get the kind of "arousal" you're looking for by using insults and anger to chastise your partner even further.

I told this to Adele, whom you'll recall was feeling sexually neglected by her husband, Jerry, and she confessed that there were times when her frustration and self-doubt would make her say things that were quite brutal. At times she would even accuse Jerry of being gay, which only reenforced his already low sense of self-worth and solidified his perception of her as a castrating woman who was causing his depression. If Adele was going to have any chance at all of helping to create an environment that would reawaken Jerry's slumbering desires, she was not going to do it with insults. Just the opposite would have to be true: Only by defusing could she maximize the chance of eliminating the anger and tension that were blocking Jerry's sexual interest. Once the tension had gone, I suggested she initiate physical contact with some gentle, nondemanding cuddles and sensuous body rubs. The rest would take care of itself.

Adele found my advice difficult to follow, because she felt threatened and hurt by Jerry's sexual neglect. But as she gradually learned to defuse from Jerry's depressed moods in other ways, she found that her hostility began to diminish in the bedroom as well. She offered to give Jerry a massage for his bad lower back one night, and one thing led to another. They became intimate for the first time in nearly five months.

On the flip side of the sex issue, however, it's also important not to use sex as a bargaining tool or weapon. I've had patients tell me that they'll withhold sex from their partners or even threaten to take their desires elsewhere in return for improvements in their loved ones' behavior. If this works, it's not working for the right reasons. Sex should be an instrument of compassion, not power. You're sacrificing what may be your best chance of all for reestablishing an intimate bond with your loved one when you use sex as a form of control. Intimacy and control are at nearly opposite ends of the emotional spectrum, and you're making a doomed choice by reaching for the latter. You may get the behavior you want from your partner, but it's very doubtful that you'll get the love.

AVOIDING THE PROVEN BOMBSHELLS: WHAT TO KEEP TO YOURSELF

You can employ all the right confrontational strategies, but there still may be issues that will set off fusion eruptions between you and your loved one no matter how diplomatically they're approached. Even the technique of moving in and moving out sometimes can cause enough friction to set off fusion.

If this is true, I suggest you simply avoid these issues. I know that this advice runs counter to most self-help counselling, which recommends leaving no stone unturned, but when you've learned that certain stones unleash a viperous snake regardless of how delicately they're touched, what sense does the touching make?

If such proven troublesome topics exist between you and your loved one, learn to deal with your feelings about them in ways other than direct discussion. Make use of support groups if you need to air grievances, and, while you don't want to fuse friends into your problems with your loved one, they're certainly good sources of support when you feel frightened or lonely.

You can talk to your loved one's therapist if he's seeing one, or talk to your own therapist if you're seeing one. You accomplish nothing by constantly fighting the same fights, and in fact only worsen your wounds. Even if the troublesome topics are vitally important to you, you must remember that getting your partner to undergo a major change, getting him to be the person *you* want him to be, should not be your goal at this stage. Your goal should be *to stop the fusion between you,* because the health of both of you depends on it.

Once the fusion is stopped, then other issues can be addressed, but not until then. Avoiding the "bombshell" topics is going to demand some masterful restraint at times, but you must realize that you're making an investment for the future when you employ this restraint. Remember, you're creating a healing environment at this point: not an ideal environment.

The ideal environment will come later, once fusion has been neutralized in your relationship. But more on that in Chapter 8.

LEARN BY THE PEACE, DON'T BE LULLED BY IT

By managing yourself and managing your partner in the ways I've outlined in these last two chapters, you will experience a much-welcomed peace. But you mustn't be lulled by this peace. Fusion is like a smoldering ember in that it can reignite at any time if sufficiently combustible situations arise.

This is especially important to keep in mind given the rate at which most types of depression can recur, even once brought under control by professional treatment. You may see "mood blips" in your loved one, which are temporary relapses capable of lasting anywhere from a few hours to a few days. Be prepared for them and don't overreact to them. They can be brought on by stress in general, or by a specific conflict in particular, so it's going to be important that you remain calm at the first sign of a downturn in your loved one's mood. If managed poorly, mood blips can lead to full-blown relapses lasting weeks or even months, so you should consider the period following your partner's recovery an important one. You must always follow the defusing rules, but walk softly and carry a compassionate stick during this period. Reacting harshly can bring your partner's depression back to full bloom.

Beware of the Good Times

But you must do more than be aware of the possibility of more "bad times" once fusion seems to be behind you—you must realize that danger lurks even in the "good times." While fusion can be contained, it also can break loose at any moment if you forget *why* it's being contained. The case of Josie, a patient of mine, illustrates this danger all too well.

Josie is a mother of two in her late thirties who had been struggling in her relationship with a chronically depressed, dysfunctional father and an overly demanding, codependent mother. She was totally fused into all the family pitfalls that her father's depression had created. She focused on how cold and uncaring he could be, and was frustrated by her manipulative mother's inability to confront the truth about how disturbed Josie's father, and their family, really was.

Josie learned to disengage and set limits. She talked to her parents less, saw them less, and created an emotional distance that allowed her breathing room. Her parents resisted, they tried to stop her defusing with guilt, with rage, and finally with threats, but she was determined to be well, and she refused to fuse with them. She set limits when they complained and pressed for more time and attention, yet she talked warmly to them when they shared feelings about other issues. But she maintained her distance.

Their relationship went through a turbulent period of adjusting to these new defusing rules, but once the adjustment was made, things got tremendously better. Josie's mother complained less and her father seemed genuinely less depressed, and the three of them began sharing much happier times.

But then Josie forgot why things had improved. As the good feelings flourished, she began seeing her parents in a more positive light. These good feelings became somewhat intoxicating for her in that they reawakened her childhood fantasies of having a loving relationship with giving, caring parents. She knew her parents had limitations, *but maybe they had changed.* Maybe they deserved a "second chance." Her expectations of them grew greater and greater, while her parents also grew more hopeful that they could finally have the loving daughter they had always wanted.

But the day of the big disappointment came quickly. Her parents started to demand more and more of her time, and Josie began dropping hints about wanting to remodel her kitchen. She was secretly hoping that her parents would offer to pay for the remodeling as a gesture of their love, while they were hoping that she would want to spend lots of time with them as a sign that she cared about their emotional needs.

I don't need to tell you the rest. A full-blown eruption occurred very shortly after Josie and her parents disappointed each other once again. Each of them blew up from the hurt and lack of caring that they believed they were experiencing from the other. The reactivity was back, and fusion was rearing its ugly head once again.

Josie and I talked about it afterward. How could she have forgotten all the defusing rules? Hadn't they worked as well as I promised?

I'll never forget her answer. "They worked almost too well," she said. "But once I had defused, I was forced to remember what a lonely and injured child I really am. Down deep I long to have a close relationship with my parents, and it's hard to use rules to suppress something like that."

I understood so well what Josie was saying. Defusing can bring losses. The losses may be real, or merely imaginary losses of what could have been, but they're losses nonetheless. What you must remember, however, is that these losses can be replaced by things of greater value, ways of relating to your loved one that will protect you from hurting each other. This may seem like a lack of intimacy at first, but only because it's new. It can develop into the deepest kind of intimacy of all, given time.

Putting It All Together: The Case of Claire and Charlie

We've covered a lot of ground in these last two chapters. We've seen how you must manage yourself as well as your partner in order to stop the fusion process. You must learn to be less sensitive to your partner's provocations, which in itself will have a calming effect, but you also must learn to discourage your partner from provoking you in the first place. There can be little hope for the future of your relationship if you do not.

Professional treatment also can help your partner get over his or her depression, as we'll be seeing in our next chapter, but in order to review your responsibilities to yourself and to your partner's recovery, I'd like to present the following case of Claire and Charlie. Claire's situation was a particularly challenging one because Charlie had an alcohol problem in addition to his dysphoric, or depressed, mood. Claire successfully responded to the challenge, however, by staying true to the strategies we've just seen. Pay close attention to Claire's experience with the fusion in her relationship, and learn by it.

Claire came to me virtually at her wit's end from trying to cope with Charlie's hotheaded, coldhearted, and always totally unpredictable behavior. He could be short-tempered one minute but sullen and long-faced the next, charming around other people but a monster around Claire. "He can come home in a good mood, but within minutes he's picking on me or one of the children for something so trivial," she told me. "It's as though he's just looking for a fight."

Dynamic and highly successful, Charlie gave the appearance of being confident almost to a fault, and yet inwardly he was extremely insecure—the result, I eventually learned, of his childhood. His father had been a heavy drinker whose only affection for his son would come in the form of sarcasm, and his mother was a self-centered and priggish woman more concerned about her place in the social register than her son's place in her heart.

As a result, alcohol had become an ego booster for Charlie, something to give him the confidence that his upbringing had not. And yet, as Claire would so graphically attest, Charlie's drinking was in fact an ego buster, a wolf in sheep's clothing that would make him irritable and mean, as he would know deep inside that nothing was being fixed but only destroyed with every drink he'd take.

As a result, Charlie's unpredictable moods and problem with alcohol became the central focus in Claire's life. If she could stop her husband from drinking, she could get started with a normal life—or at least that was her thinking.

But Charlie, needless to say, didn't take a similar view. He saw Claire's concern as a meddlesome cover-up for the simple fact that she had nothing else better to do with her life. And in a way, unfortunately, he was right. Claire had not trained for any sort of self-supporting career, and having been raised by an abusive, alcoholic father herself, she had very low self-esteem, just like Charlie.

But these self-doubts, of course, only fueled her concern over Charlie's drinking. She felt totally dependent on him, so he *had* to get well. Sometimes she would retreat when he attacked her, but more often she would stand up for herself and call Charlie a loser and a drunk. This would only backfire, however, as Charlie would storm off to the bar, where he'd drink even more as a way of licking his wounds.

Claire and Charlie were as fused as a couple can be. Every action from Claire would produce a negative reaction from Charlie, which would invite yet another action from Claire. And squeezing the fusion vice even tighter was Claire's belief that her well-being hinged on Charlie's well-being. She felt she was fighting for her life, and yet—as is always the case with fusion—she was ruining her life in the process.

When I explained this to Claire, she had trouble understanding it at first. How else was she going to show Charlie her concern? She couldn't just stand idly by and watch him destroy himself. His drinking was bad for him, bad for her and the kids.

And it wasn't as though she hadn't tried to get him to go for professional help. "He just tells me that my nagging is what makes him drink, and that if I'd stop, he'd be fine. Well, I did stop for a while, and things weren't fine. Nothing changed. Nothing ever changes. What am I supposed to do?"

I told Claire she was correct to assume her husband had an alcohol problem, and probably an underlying depression that was contributing to it, but I also had to tell her that I agreed with Charlie that she was doing a poor job of handling the situation. She resisted, she squirmed, she challenged me to say that her reactions to Charlie weren't normal.

"Normal, yes. But helpful, no," was my reply. I went on to explain how her extreme emotional involvement with Charlie's problem was giving it the very sort of "charge" that was causing it to rage on with such uncontrollable force. She was going to have to pull the plug on this charge by backing away, disengaging, becoming self-sufficient and independent of Charlie in ways that would force him to see his drinking problem for what it really was.

"Neither of you is giving each other the distance you need to see this thing for what it is," I told her. "If we're correct, and Charlie is both alcoholic and depressed, then we're dealing with two serious medical problems that need to be seen as just that—medical problems. Would you be in your current state of mind if Charlie were battling cancer right now? You need to see his drinking and his mood disturbance in the same way."

That said, we agreed that Claire would start showing less passion and more compassion, that she would be willing to participate in treatment with Charlie, but that she would also work toward being less emotionally involved. No more impassioned pleas, no more furious threats, no more roof-raising arguments. Their fighting was doing nothing more than further upsetting both of them. She was going to focus on managing herself—on building a base of support outside the relationship and a base of confidence inside herself by pursuing work activities and regular exercise routines.

And if her husband's behavior would not improve?

Then she calmly would have to face some difficult decisions, which, as we'll see in Chapter 7, might include a readiness to leave the relationship or to lead a fully parallel life.

Charlie reacted as I had suspected he would. Without his wife's oppressive censoring, he had no one but himself to blame for his bad moods and drunkenness. For the first time he found himself totally alone in his depression, and it frightened him. Approximately two weeks into Claire's disengagement from him, he broke down in tears and was able to share how truly alone and terrified he felt.

Claire responded by confessing that her own fears and insecurities had been responsible for her overinvolvement with his problems in the first place. She was deeply sorry for that, but she was also firmly convinced that he had a serious alcohol problem as well as a depression, which were not going to get better unless he agreed to receive professional help.

"I have the right to live a well-adjusted life, and that means having a healthy marriage with someone who is rational enough to realize when he needs help with something he can't handle," she firmly announced. "I love you, but I can't live with you if you're going to continue to destroy yourself. If I were to continue to live with you this way, then I'd be just as responsible for our unhappiness as you."

Charlie was in my office the following week.

I've streamlined the case of Claire and Charlie, because although it worked out well in the end, it was rough going to get there. It took Claire several months to gather the courage and self-confidence to confront Charlie, and for several weeks he continued and even escalated his abusive ways when he perceived her growing independence as a threat. Such resistance, however, is what you must be prepared to face. Immense forces are at work to push you and your loved one into the fusion process in the first place, so considerable force also is going to be needed to pull you free.

Next on the agenda: What you can expect and what your loved one can expect to gain by seeking professional help.

THE ROLE OF
PROFESSIONAL HELP

"For extreme illnesses, extreme treatments are
most fitting."

HIPPOCRATES, 460–400 B.C.

Someone can sleep until noon because of a physical illness,
and no judgment gets passed on the person's character.

But sleep until noon because of feeling depressed, and judg-
ments get passed left and right.

"You're just being lazy."

"Stop being such an escapist."

"You're drinking too much."

"It's all in your head."

And of course, it *is* all in the person's head, and that's
precisely the problem. A depressive disorder is just what it says
it is—a "dis-order" of the normal functioning of the brain, often
biological in nature, and hence no more deliberate or reprehen-
sible than a disorder of any other organ of the body.

124

It is important for you to keep this in mind as you read this chapter. Highly effective medical and psychological treatments are available to help both you and your loved one with the depression that you face, but the treatment must be sought with an open and nonjudgmental mind. No one should be thought of as "weak" for seeking such help, but rather strong for having the courage to face the reality that the help is needed. There is no shame in having illness or despair, yet fear, prejudice, and ignorance still dominate our view.

If you sincerely feel that your current relationship difficulties can be worked out on your own using the strategies I've outlined in the preceding two chapters, more power to you. You're very fortunate that the fusion in your relationship has not progressed beyond the self-help level. But if you have your doubts, please show the sense and the strength to make the next step and enlist the help of a health professional. This applies to you as well as for your loved one. The contagious aspects of your partner's condition may have affected you to a point where you, as much as he or she, would benefit from psychiatric treatment. Remember, too, that by helping yourself you also help your partner, so you needn't feel selfish for doing virtually everything possible to be as healthy and as happy as you can.

I'd like to begin this chapter with the case of a couple that would have been doomed had the appropriate professional treatment not finally been found.

The Case of the Pot Calling the Kettle Black

I've treated some unusual cases in my fifteen years as a psychiatrist, but few as challenging as Shirley's. Shirley, a retired school teacher in her mid-sixties, came to me after having seen six other doctors and therapists over a period of four years. She was beginning to think herself a "lost cause," and it didn't take long for me to see why.

Shirley suffered from an obsessive/compulsive disorder that caused her to fear that she had left matches or sharp objects such as pins, needles, or razor blades in places where they might do someone harm. For forty-five minutes we discussed how irrational her fear was, how it dominated her life, how it made her irritable and depressed, and how she was determined to get over it this time, "no matter what."

Yet what did Shirley do as she went to leave my office after that first meeting?

She hesitated at the door, and with sadness in her eyes returned to make a quick inspection of my wastebasket, pencil cup, and even planter. "I couldn't have slept tonight," she said with a sense of defeat.

I was not surprised to learn in my next meeting with Shirley that her problem had been a source of considerable conflict with her husband, Mike, over the years. I asked to see Mike when I heard this, and I'm glad I did. Mike told me that he considered his wife to be "totally off her rocker," that it was not unusual for her to get him up in the middle of the night to make him rummage through garbage bags and baskets of dirty laundry. "She drives me nuts," he said.

I don't think Mike knew how much truth there was to his words. Here was a man acting in a totally irrational manner, sifting through garbage in the middle of the night with rubber gloves, yet considering his wife to be the one with the screws loose. It was one of the most glaring examples of the "contagious-emotions" phenomenon—of one person's behavior "infecting" the behavior of another—that I had ever seen.

"But Mike," I said. "Can't you see that you're validating and even perpetuating your wife's problem with every wastebasket you overturn? You're giving her reason to believe there might be some merit to her fears after all."

But of course Mike had lost the ability to see it that way. Fusion had pulled him so close to his wife's problem that he no longer had the perspective to think or act in a rational manner. Even more critical, he had relinquished responsibility for his actions. His remark that he was merely doing what any "normal" person would do in a similar situation told me that he had become a virtual pawn of his wife's problem. He had fused with Shirley's condition to a point where it had taken control over his life. And by doing so, unfortunately, he had only made life worse for both of them.

But the real topper came when I remarked to Shirley in my second session with her that her husband must be quite a nice guy to be forever pilfering through the trash for her.

"Are you kidding? He's a miserable SOB," she told me. "He's irritable and moody, and he makes me so nervous. My problem has gotten worse in the two years since he retired, because now he's around the house bitching at me all day."

And there I had it. No wonder Shirley had failed with her other treatments. No one had realized that treating her was treating only half the problem. The anxiety that was causing her obsessive/compulsive problem was being intensified and perpetuated by the fusion that existed between her and her husband. Her problem was not going to go away until that fusion went away—I was convinced of that—so I suggested to Shirley that my treatment of her include treatment of Mike.

And sure enough, my meetings with Mike told me that the years of turmoil had taken their toil. He suffered from mood disturbances that probably predated his involvement with Shirley's problem, but the tendencies understandably had been brought to full bloom by the strain of having to deal with his wife's bizarre behavior. The two had been growing steadily sicker together for over twenty years—yet only Shirley had come to the attention of the medical community.

The Help You May Need

We'll be returning to Mike and Shirley at the end of this chapter so that I can tell you how I "miraculously" helped them over their problem, but the point I wish to make here is that your partner's recovery may require that *you*, and not just he, participate in the therapy process. If you and your partner have been fused for an appreciable period of time—approximately a year or longer—it's very likely that you also are emotionally unwell. I'm not saying that you're as disturbed as your partner, but I am saying that the fusion has probably inflicted you with emotional wounds.

This raises an unavoidable truth regarding your loved one's chances of getting well. Even if he or she agrees to undergo the finest treatment available, the treatment may not be enough unless *your* contributions to the fusion process are also addressed. Just as Mike unintentionally was thwarting Shirley's recovery, you could be guilty of a similar kind of therapy obstruction. Yes, the self-management and partner-management strategies we discussed in Chapters 4 and 5 can do a great deal to curb your contributions to the fusion process, but they might not be enough if you've been wounded by fusion that has been especially extreme or long-standing. The strategies also may be insufficient if you, like Mike, have emotional problems that existed prior to your current relationship difficulties.

But how can you know if therapy would help you?

Rarely is it a cut-and-dried issue, but my years of experience have shown me that there are certain key symptoms to look for. If one or more of these symptoms could be said to describe your current mental state, then modern psychiatric treatments could probably help you.

1. *You feel depressed or worried and anxious almost all of the time.* Feeling upset immediately following a fusion outburst is one thing, but feeling upset on an ongoing basis is another. If your feelings of sadness and/or worry are chronic, those feelings are definitely contributing to the fusion process and must be treated if your relationship with your loved one is going to improve.

2. *You've lost the ability to control your anger.* Feeling angry is unavoidable, but if you find that you cannot control *showing* your anger, you may be suffering from an underlying anxiety

disorder. It's no reason to feel bad, because an estimated twenty million Americans are in the same boat, but it's important to get help for your problem because there can be no chance of stopping the fusion between you and your loved one until you do. And don't hide behind the excuse that "anyone" would react as angrily as you do to your partner's provocations. That's a rationalization, not a solution.

3. *You make unrealistic demands for intimacy.* By unrealistic, I mean that you insist on emotional support from your partner even though you know he or she is not capable of giving it. This is a guaranteed fusion catalyst, and could be a sign that you suffered from a lack of emotional support as a child. You desperately want what you never had, yet it's very possible that you would not be able to deal with the intimacy you crave even if your partner were to give it. This is especially apt to be true if one or both of your parents were alcoholic, abusive, or in some way emotionally disturbed. You may not know how to handle intimacy, because you've never known it, yet you demand it because you think it's owed to you. If this is the case, you need to find out—for your own good as well as the good of your relationship. Therapy can help you.

4. *You're experiencing physical ailments.* When the mind feels overburdened, the body often feels the pain. Chronic headaches, backache, stomach or intestinal problems, sexual dysfunction, or excessive fatigue—all can be signs that the stress of your fused relationship is exceeding your capacity to cope. If you're having such problems, don't feel you're being a "head case" to consider your relationship difficulties as the cause. It's going to be important for you to feel well physically if you're going to be able to stand up emotionally to the challenges that coping with your partner will present.

5. *You are being subjected to suicidal blackmail.* This occurs when your loved one makes repeated threats or actual attempts at taking his life, and it's such a stress to you—as well as a danger to your loved one—that you mustn't try to deal with it

on your own. There's simply too much at stake. Suicidal black-mail can be such an upsetting and sadistic game, and such a potent instigator of fusion in its ability to totally dominate your mental state, that it absolutely must be policed by a professional.

Clearing the Path

Deciding to see a therapist to help you deal with your current situation may not be an easy decision to make. You may feel you're "giving in," being weak, or accepting the "sick role." After all, isn't your depressed partner the one you should be shipping off to the shrink?

If you're having doubts about seeking professional help for yourself, let me assuage those doubts with this: Your decision to enlist professional guidance to help you with your problems could be the most important thing you can do to help your partner. Not only will it help stop the fusion that's making his or her condition worse, it will help clear the path for him to seek treatment of his own. I've seen this so often in my own practice. The avenue by which I finally get to see the depressed person who so desperately needs my help is the depressed person's partner. The visits by the partner remove the stigma, the fear, and the threat.

This was the case with Karen and Paul, the couple we met back in Chapter 3 who were plagued by Paul's triple addiction to marijuana, alcohol, and exercise. Paul was extremely resistant to seeking help for his problems. Even when I finally did get to see him, he smoked a joint right before the session and later smirked that he was sure I couldn't detect any change in his behavior. That's how defiant he was initially.

And yet it was Karen's willingness to see me that had opened the door for this all-important initial visit from Paul in the first place. As harshly skeptical as he appeared on the surface, he saw positive changes taking place in Karen as a result of her sessions with me, and he was intrigued—perhaps even threatened—by them. "I'm here mainly because my wife thinks I should be," was his explanation to me during that first visit. "It fascinates me that you guys can be so presumptuous as to believe you can fix the way somebody actually thinks."

Yet that's precisely what I was able to do with Paul in just a little over six months' time, but not without his help and the help of the AA groups he attends. He remains amazed to this day at how his multiple addictions had been altering his brain chemistry and depressing his mood. These chemical changes had also falsely colored his thinking and blurred his vision of reality. He remarked to me in one of our last sessions, in fact, that he felt as though he had received a "brain transplant." The irony is that his biggest remorse was that he had waited so long to get help. But without his wife's help, who knows if he would ever have been ready?

Putting Fusion First

Not all my patients enjoy epiphanies as remarkable as Paul's, though I must say that I do see my share of major turnarounds. It constantly reminds me of just how "physical" an organ the brain really is. Yes, its job is the seemingly magical one of directing our consciousness, but it goes about this task in a fashion that is more mechanical—and hence "repairable"— than some people care to think.

We'll be talking more about this in the section on psychiatric medications later in this chapter, but for now I need to make an important point regarding professional help and fusion. It's very possible that the therapist you or your partner sees may not be privy to the fusion concept. Worse yet, he or she may inadvertently contribute to the fusion between you and your loved one if he allows you to dwell too heavily on your partner's disturbed behavior during your therapy sessions.

Overinvolvement with your loved one's troubles is much of the reason you're in your current situation in the first place, remember, so you mustn't dwell even further on your partner as part of your "recovery" process. To do so will be a step in exactly the opposite direction from gaining the kind of independence and self-esteem that will free you from fusion and help you regain control of your life.

This isn't to say your loved one's condition must be off-limits entirely—it is, after all, a major source of stress in your life—but to focus on your partner's problems at the expense of your own is what you must avoid. If your therapist is good, he or she should know this whether he's aware of my fusion concept or not. But if he doesn't—it's going to be up to you to play teacher. Explain the concept of fusion as best you can, or let your therapist see a copy of this book. That may seem self-serving for me to say, but I do it only because I feel so strongly that fusion is an important "missing link" in the way depression currently is being treated in this country. Fusion must be stopped if the destructive consequences of depression are going to be stopped, and this holds as true in the therapist's office as it does in the home.

Getting Your Partner to Receive Help

But your greatest challenge of all, of course, will be to get your depressed loved one to undergo treatment. Yes, it's possible that his or her depression could run its course and "burn out" on its own within six to eight months. And it's also possible that his or her depressed behavior isn't true depression at all, but rather only a symptom of a character disorder, alcoholism, a drug addiction, or a compulsive problem such as uncontrollable gambling or an eating disorder.

A good therapist, however, is far better qualified than you to make that kind of diagnosis. So even if depression turns out not to be your partner's primary problem, professional help can be of great value merely for telling you what is, and what to do about it. At least you'll know what you're up against, and that in itself can be a great relief.

"But he just won't consider it. He's so nuts that he even had a T-shirt made that says NO SHRINKING ALLOWED. He makes fun of psychiatry, and says it's a huge waste of money."

Those were Karen's words to me as she faced the seemingly impossible task of convincing her husband, Paul, he needed treatment. But we finally got him to agree, as you know, and here's how we did it.

THE EDUCATIONAL APPROACH

I first advised Karen to appeal to Paul's sense of reason, or what little was left of it, by explaining that the brain was an organ that could get "sick" just like any other organ of the body. His illness, consequently, was no more his "fault" than developing diabetes would be his fault. If he was to be blamed for anything, it would be for refusing to receive treatment and allowing his illness to spread to people he loved. I also advised Karen to inform Paul that he could expect about a 75 to 85 percent chance of being cured of his depression if he stopped using drugs and alcohol and that the costs of his treatment would probably be partially covered by his medical insurance.

But Paul didn't buy it for the simple reason that he refused to admit he was sick. So I had Karen play tougher the next time with tack number two—the confrontational approach.

THE CONFRONTATIONAL APPROACH

The confrontational approach is less educational than personal. You begin with an apology for whatever degradation and hurt you may have caused your loved one during your fused struggles. You were just instinctively trying to protect yourself, and it wasn't your intention to be malicious. This apology also should include an admission that you have emotional problems of your own and that you've been just as much to blame for the fusion between you as your loved one.

After making these concessions, however, you must get

tougher, I told Karen. You must stand up for your right to live a well-adjusted life—an important part of which is a feeling of hope about the future. Yes, you will do everything possible to help your loved one through his troubled time, but what you *cannot* do is stand by and watch your loved one—and your relationship—continue to deteriorate. It's simply too upsetting and too unhealthy for you to live or relate closely with someone who is emotionally disturbed and refuses to try to get well.

"But I am trying, and this is my medicine," Paul said sardonically as he poured himself another glass of wine.

Where was Karen to go from there?

If Karen had been independent enough—financially as well as emotionally—I'd have told her to pack her bags with the announcement that she wasn't returning until Paul either had cured himself or was undergoing treatment. Karen was not in that position, however, just as you may not be, so the alternative is what I call the emotional embargo.

THE EMOTIONAL EMBARGO: WIDENING THE EMOTIONAL DISTANCE

Continuing to struggle with someone who refuses to take responsibility for his or her own emotional health is as poisonous as it is pointless, so you must simply sever your emotional ties by defusing. Yes, you may continue to live in the same house, but there will be minimal interaction and the areas that have been sources of conflict between you and your partner will be off limits entirely—your emotional distance will be quite wide.

Announce this to your loved one as calmly, but also as compassionately, as possible. You don't want it to sound like a threat, nor will it be successful if you merely do it out of anger or desperation. Rather, you must see this action only as the most healthy response you are capable of making to the sad reality that your partner has brought to bear. Unless your loved one gets professional help, he or she has left you with no choice but to leave the relationship entirely or to take your emotions and your energies elsewhere, somewhere where they can be free of the contagious elements of his self-destruction and despair.

Once you've said this, you need never say it again. But you also must follow through. You must sever all the emotional ties that cause you to feel unsafe or provoked, and thus make yourself "fusion proof." Only then is your loved one going to experience the kind of extreme isolation that may be required for him finally to realize he needs help.

You also should present your loved one with a list of phone numbers (I suggest two or three) of doctors he can call if and when he should decide to reach out for help. This may seem incidental, but it is not. The "moment of truth" that your loved one experiences during his isolation may be very short, and if he cannot react to it quickly, it may pass before he can take action. It's important not to let this happen. By having access to professional resources, your loved one will be able to capitalize on his moment of awareness as soon as it strikes.

This, in fact, is the way Paul finally came to see the light. Karen's job of constructing an emotional quarantine had been masterful. She would be cordial, but never warm. She also started pursuing outside interests and rekindling old friend-ships—creating a life outside the house. And yes, she extended her embargo to the bedroom. That was her choice, because she felt it would be too emotionally unsafe for her to relate to Paul in this intimate and vulnerable manner.

Paul was able to deal with Karen's detachment for a while. He professed to enjoy it, in fact, as the "bitch" was finally off his back. But within about a week he started to see things dif-ferently. Without Karen to blame for his rebellious behavior, he was forced to view that behavior in a different light. Who was he rebelling against now—himself?

But he wasn't going to give in without a fight. His drinking and pot smoking and grueling exercise routine were his friends, his only friends now that Karen had pulled away, so he was going to embrace them more closely than ever. His drinking escalated from a quart of wine a night to nearly a half gallon, and he started smoking two joints instead of one, and his daily workout went from ninety minutes to two hours.

And yet the more closely he did cling to his "friends," the more he could see that they were not his friends at all. They were his enemies, and they had been all along. They were costing him the things that were most dear to him—his wife and his children and his ability to think with an outstanding, creative mind. His life was becoming one unbearable guilt-ridden fog, from which he finally realized he had to escape.

And that's when it hit him that he needed help. His once pleasurable world suddenly had become a very painful world, yet he was addicted to it. His addictions no longer gave him pleasure—they caused him immense guilt, in fact—yet he had become physically as well as psychologically dependent on them. He had created quite a little hell for himself, which he didn't know how to escape.

This all descended on Paul one Monday morning as he lay in bed with his usual hangover. Finally he knew something had to change. He didn't know what, or how, or how quickly, but he felt so low and so lost that he knew he had to ask for help. He found the piece of paper with my phone number on it which he had thrown in the wastebasket by his bed and gave my office a call. The most difficult first step had been made.

WHAT NOT TO DO

Karen succeeded in getting Paul to undergo treatment because she obeyed one cardinal rule of the defusion process: she let distance do the talking. By pulling away from Paul, she left him with no one to confront but himself.

You must remain aware of this "distance talks louder than involvement" rule as you're tempted to succumb to the frustration that the defusion process sometimes can cause. Hold your ground and be patient—it might take a while! By jumping back into the turmoil with your loved one you only become another log for the fusion fire. Especially important to avoid are:

Pleading: Pleading is a tactic born out of desperation, and stems more from fear of your own inadequacies than a sincere desire to help your loved one. While it may work for some people, in general your loved one will pick up on your desperation and use it to reinforce his belief that *you* are the sicker of the two of you. This, in turn, will make it even easier for him to deny his emotional problems—so please avoid pleading at all costs.

Manipulating: By manipulating, I mean making threats (i.e., frequently saying that you're leaving for good and then returning after a few hours or days), overdramatizing (i.e., your loved one belongs in a straitjacket or a nursing home), or trying to take control behind your partner's back (i.e., by booking psychiatric consultations without his consent). These tactics, like pleading, only will show your desperation, increase fusion, and further allow your loved one to view you as the greater troublemaker in your relationship.

Best Treatments to Seek

So the time has come. You or your loved one has decided to see a therapist, or perhaps you've decided to see one together. But what type of therapist do you see? Do you go to a psychiatrist, who's also an M.D.? Or do you opt for a psychologist who holds a Ph.D.? Or perhaps go to see a marriage counselor, licensed therapist, or social worker?

I'm going to answer that question as simply and as non-controversially as possible. More important than the academic degree of the therapist you see is the experience that professional has with diagnosing and treating mood disturbances. And rather than worry about *whom* you see, you should concentrate on *why* you're seeing him. As long as you have a reasonable understanding of the problems you and your loved one face, and you have specific goals for what you expect from your therapy, you should be able to find a qualified health professional to handle your case. But you must be your own advocate—don't be afraid to ask questions and evaluate the professional's approach.

Even if you start with someone who doesn't have the qualifications to prescribe the psychiatric medications that may be needed, simply ask whether he or she will be able to refer you to someone who does. The important thing to remember in your first experience with psychological treatment is that it can work only if *you* also are willing to work. You will be disappointed if your expectations are for a push-button cure.

That being said, let's look now at the types of therapy I feel are best suited for treating depression in general and fusion in particular. Many kinds are available, but rather than confuse you with an extensive overview, I'm going to focus on what I feel can be most effective against the kinds of problems we've been addressing in this book. If you feel you would still like additional information at the conclusion of this section, write or call the National Institute of Mental Health in Maryland and request their educational materials for the specific issues that concern you or your loved one.

PSYCHOTHERAPY

The term "psychotherapy" scares a lot of people because they think it requires years of painful probing into the psyche. However, you mustn't confuse psychotherapy with psychoanalysis. Psychoanalysis may be the "root canal" of psychiatry, whereas psychotherapy is the filling. Psychotherapy addresses thoughts and behaviors as they occur in the present, and deals much less with the unconscious, "Freudian" reasons for these thoughts and behaviors.

Psychotherapy also can be administered by therapists who have very different levels of training. Seeing an M.D. will be necessary for the prescribing of medications, but not for undergoing psychotherapy. Highly specialized psychotherapies, moreover, have been proven through extensive research to be effective in treating depression, and are also known to be helpful for other mood disorders such as obsessive/compulsive behavior, phobias, anxiety, and panic attacks. These specialized therapies come in two basic forms.

COGNITIVE/BEHAVIORAL THERAPY

The fundamental belief of cognitive therapy is that most depressions are caused by distorted, negative perceptions of the self and of the world. These perceptions often go on to fulfill their own prophecies by influencing the depressed person's behavior in ways that bring his negative expectations about. Someone who feels unliked and anticipates having a bad time at a party, for example, usually will behave in ways that produce precisely what he expects.

Cognitive therapy seeks to correct this kind of negative thinking by challenging it and proving it wrong. A cognitive behavioral therapist might also suggest changes in behavior to help dispel negative thoughts—ways for the depressed person to take more responsibility for his environment and his life. This assists the depressed person in overcoming the helplessness he may feel as it also builds self-esteem. Cognitive therapy (called cognitive/behavioral therapy if cognitive and behavioral techniques are combined) is an excellent treatment for mild to moderate depressions and can be done individually, together with your partner, or even in groups.

INTERPERSONAL THERAPY

Where cognitive therapy focuses on faulty perceptions of the self and the world, interpersonal therapy looks for faulty relationship patterns—mistakes the depressed person makes in dealing with other people. Such mistakes can create loneliness, despair, stress, and low self-esteem—all the ingredients depression is made of—and yet they are so correctable if better ways of interpersonal communication are learned. Many of the principles of interpersonal therapy are similar to the self-management and partner-management skills we looked at in Chapters 4 and 5. They teach people how to relate to one another in ways that are *con*structive rather than *de*structive, that permit true feelings to come through rather than self-protective facades. Like cognitive therapy, interpersonal therapy is excellent for treating mild to moderate depressions and can be conducted effectively by a wide range of therapists. Unlike cognitive therapy, however, it usually is done on an individual basis only.

I do believe that some chronic depressions, in particular, need to be treated with individual psychotherapy that looks more closely at early life experiences, but your therapist should be able to tell you if such additional insight-oriented counseling is going to be needed. Psychiatric medications may be necessary—but again, these are determinations that can be made as their need becomes known. Cognitive and interpersonal therapy are both excellent starting points for getting recovery from depression under way.

FAMILY THERAPY

When parents become fused, children also feel the heat. This isn't to say that every child exposed to fusion will be "burned" to the point of needing psychological help, but some will, and it's important to be sensitive to the possibility. If one or more of your children are having emotional, disciplinary, or scholastic problems, individual therapy for the child and family counseling should strongly be considered.

Family therapy can help redefine each member's appropriate role within the family—something that may have become clouded by the fusion process. It also can help everyone realize that each family member has his limitations, which must be accepted realistically. Arguing over such limitations does nothing but separate family members even further by increasing fusion. Perhaps most important of all, however, family therapy can show children that they are not to blame for their parents' troubles. This is important for their current emotional health, as well as for the future.

MARITAL (CONJOINT) THERAPY

As I mentioned earlier in this chapter, fusion may not be a term that will strike a familiar note to many therapists regardless of the type or amount of training they have received. This need not be a problem, however, because most good therapists will conduct their sessions with an understanding of fusion that is intuitive, if not by conscious design. Most psychological disciplines understand that to be happy with anyone else, you must first be happy with yourself. This is the fundamental principle for dissipating fusion—so trust me when I say that most therapists will conduct their sessions in a manner consistent with my "defusion" strategies.

This may not be true, however, with some therapists. So much emphasis has been put on "communicating" and "negotiating" in relationships in the past two decades that many marriage counselors unwittingly *contribute* to fusion by encouraging couples to "talk through" their difficulties, no matter what.

I'm going to have to take issue with that approach, and my reason for doing so is quite specific. Arousal only begets more arousal, which clouds the powers of reason. Worse yet, the literal content of most arguments is not really relevant to what needs to be addressed. What needs to be addressed is the process of fusion which causes couples to find things to argue about in the first place. It's not that Harry leaves wet towels on the bed, it's that he's self-centered and neglectful of his wife's emotional needs, and she is unable to express or take responsibility for those needs except by yelling about the towels. I'm not saying that marital therapy can't be an effective technique for helping marital woes, but I am saying that it must be done skillfully and with an understanding of fusion forces. When I treat a couple, it's my practice first to see the couple together and assess how severe the fusion is between them. If I consider it not too serious, I instruct them on how to "defuse" using the strategies outlined in Chapters 4 and 5, and I continue to see them as a couple. We work through the defusion process week by week, and usually within several months they're back on a healthy track.

If I deem the fusion in a marriage severe, however, I take a different tack. After a few joint sessions, I begin to see the partners individually. This helps by creating some distance between them as it also encourages the kind of independent thinking that the long-term success of the defusion process requires. Once their arousal levels have been calmed, and they've learned to take responsibility for their contributions to the fusion process, I start seeing them as a couple again while continuing to conduct individual sessions. Gradually I wean the number of individual sessions down as fusion lessens, and we spend more time in the joint sessions, where an acceptable relationship is finally worked out. We work on coordinating needs for intimacy and establishing realistic goals for what the relationship can and cannot be.

The Therapeutic Separation

There are times when even my best efforts fail, and a couple will continue to fuse both in my office and at home. In these cases, I frequently will recommend what I call a "therapeutic separation." Properly managed, it can be a veritable lifesaver for marriages that otherwise would be doomed.

A therapeutic separation is most suited for couples who are so fused that while they cannot live together, they cannot live apart. First and foremost, the separation teaches them that they can survive alone. This reduces much of the fear that was fueling the fusion. Once the fear has receded and the fusion is gone, they can look at their relationship more objectively. Quite often this leads to the conclusion that although their relationship has its problems, it's worth saving. Not without separating, however, would such a realization be possible. Many couples need to get away from each other in order to gain the perspective and insight needed to understand where their relationship has gone wrong.

I usually recommend that such separations last from three to six months and that they begin with an initial stage during which no communication at all is allowed. This maximizes the chance for individual growth and self-understanding, as it also heightens the realization of what life would be like should the relationship end. I also recommend that each member of the couple undergo therapy for the duration of the separation, so that their thoughts and feelings can be properly analyzed and understood.

Separations that are not supervised by a therapist can be risky, as neither partner may gain a sense of independence. This can lead to a permanent separation and flight to yet another destructive relationship, or to a series of separations and reconciliations, without providing help to either partner or stability to the relationship.

Guided properly, however, the therapeutic separation sometimes can be a veritable miracle cure for couples whose fusion otherwise would be terminal. Even just the mention of such separations sometimes can have an immediate healing effect. A couple can be deep in the throes of fusion, threatening divorce with nearly every word, but quickly become as calm as kittens the minute I propose my separation scheme. The anger lifts, and we suddenly have a much clearer view of the fears, reservations, and even love that really exist. I offer the case of Mark and Susan as an example of just how effective a properly supervised therapeutic separation can be.

Mark is a successful 56-year-old stockbroker whose marriage to Susan, 45, is the second one for each of them. They came to me because Mark was acting irritable and depressed, which had caused Susan to lose sexual interest in him. This understandably was making Mark's depression worse—clearly an advanced fusion scenario.

Mark had tried antidepressant medication with another doctor, and the two had even undergone sex therapy to rekindle Susan's flames, but neither had worked. Susan went so far as to warn me that she feared their case might be "hopeless," but I didn't let that distract me, because I picked up on something in our very first meeting that I felt was crucial.

There was intense anger—it pervaded the office. They weren't just disappointed in each other, they were intensely angry, and I could see it in everything they said. Their marriage had seemed to have so much promise early on—great sex, great communication, lots of common interests and goals—but in time the dazzle dimmed, and Mark's moods grew darker and darker.

It was never clear whether his depression preceded the marital problems or caused them, but that's the nature of fusion. They found themselves arguing over trivialities, taking each other's idiosyncrasies personally, and hearing insults where none had been intended. The bickering escalated over a period of about two years until it erupted into full-fledged fusion, rife with shouting matches, extended stays in the guest room, and frequent threats of divorce. Even in the safety of my office, the arguments would flare up quite often.

"All he wants is sex, Doctor. We were alone in the living room the other night and I was trying to tell him about a problem I was having with our son, and he starts stroking my thigh. All he cares about is getting laid."

"I was trying to comfort her, for Christ's sake. But she'll use anything to put me off. She bitches that I'm withdrawn and that she's not getting enough attention or support, but then does everything she can to push me away. How do you think I feel having to beg for sex from my own wife? I could be getting more action if I were single!"

"So why not try it—it'd be a relief for both of us!" Susan quipped.

And that's how those first few sessions went. I was able to find a more effective antidepressant for Mark, and his mood improved considerably, but nothing much changed between them. There was nothing but blame. Everything was always the other person's fault. There was never any sharing of the situation they had created—and hence there could be no solution. I saw a separation as our only chance for gaining the calmer perspective their relationship was going to need to let go of its heat.

They both seemed surprised at my suggestion, but each was too proud, of course, to back down from what I proposed— after all, each of them had been threatening divorce for months. After several weeks of arguing over who was going to stay in the house, we agreed that they would take an apartment and alternate their stays a week at a time. We also agreed that the ground rules for their separation would be as follows:

- ▲ no dating others for at least three months
- ▲ no contact, or minimal contact, with each other for four to eight weeks
- ▲ ample time spent alone to contemplate their own personal thoughts and feelings and to generate a vision of their own lives
- ▲ effort put toward bolstering friendships and work relationships so that greater feelings of independence could be gained
- ▲ continued therapy—individually—so that their progress could be checked

And how did they make out?

Within about a month, I could see in my individual sessions with Mark and Susan that their hostilities toward each other were decreasing significantly, and that each was beginning to take more responsibility for their contributions to the fusion that had existed between them. When I felt sufficient progress had been made in that area, I suggested they start seeing each other once a week or so to discuss what they had been learning about themselves. I also suggested they share the visions of life they had been having during the separation period.

And to each one's surprise, these visions were not as exclusive of one another as either would have predicted just two months earlier. They had more love, more common needs, and more respect for each other than the fusion between them had allowed them to realize. Their weekly meetings soon turned into weekly "dates," romance returned to their relationship, and they eventually decided to give their marriage a second try. Today they're at peace with each other, they know how to recognize and manage fusion, and they've stopped blaming each other for a relationship that may occasionally fall short of being ideal. They're "happy" by each of their assessments, and very thankful that I was able to guide the separation that brought their happiness about.

The Role of Medication Therapy: Just Say "Yes"

Four years ago, Bruce's life was a roller-coaster ride through hell itself. He was either so "up" that he'd lose touch with reality, or so "down" that he couldn't face reality. When he was up, he went on shopping sprees, drank heavily, and couldn't sleep for days. When he was down, he felt overwhelmed by despair and hopelessness, and couldn't get out of bed. There were periods of middle ground for Bruce, but they never lasted.

Finally, in a desperate attempt to escape, he took a serious overdose. Thankfully, he was discovered in time and survived. Bruce suffered from manic-depressive illness, and I'm convinced he would not be alive today had he not literally been "saved" by a psychiatric drug called Lithium. He leads a totally normal life today and is a very talented person who is an asset to his family and community.

Psychiatric drugs are not just for cases as extreme as Bruce's however. They can be the small difference that can make a *huge* difference in a wide variety of less extreme emotional disorders.

"But aren't they just a crutch, Doctor, a way of masking the symptoms that doesn't really get to their cause?"

Those were Mike's words to me (you'll remember Mike as the nervous husband of Shirley, whom we met at the beginning of this chapter) when I suggested he try Xanax, an antianxiety medication, to help him deal with his wife's problem.

"But, Mike," I answered him, "when you're dealing with fusion, the symptoms somtimes *are* the cause."

I went on to use Mike's own situation as an example. Yes, his irritability was a symptom of an underlying mood disturbance that would need to be treated with both medicine and psychotherapy, but his irritability was also the *cause* of the fusion that existed between him and his wife. It was contributing to the anxiety that was causing Shirley to behave in her obsessive-compulsive fashion. Her behavior, in turn, was making Mike even more irritable—which was making Shirley even more compulsive. It was a classic fusion cycle that was going to have to be broken at some point, and I saw Mike's anxiety as the most approachable place to do it. I also would need to treat Shirley's obsessive-compulsive disorder directly, of course, but calming Mike's side of the fusion seesaw was going to be an important part of a comprehensive plan to help both of them.

Mike understood my logic, but he still resisted the anti-anxiety medication. "Legal or not, it's a drug, and I might get hooked. Besides, it just doesn't seem right to take something that affects the brain."

I could sympathize with Mike, because his reaction was one that I get quite often. People can be reluctant to take medication for the brain, yet they have no reservations at all about taking a medication for the heart, lungs, liver, pancreas, skin, or any other organ of the body. Is it because we think the brain should somehow be "above" becoming disordered? That its incredible intricacy should somehow protect it from malfunctioning?

That intricacy only makes it more susceptible to glitches, unfortunately, just as any machine becomes more prone to breakdown the greater its number of moving parts. We must stop viewing the brain as so invulnerable or so mystical that it should be capable of "fixing" itself if and when it does break down. Yet that is the implication of these attitudes.

"In terms of its complexity, the brain makes every other organ of the body look about as complicated as a wheel," I told Mike. "And it doesn't take much for some very minor problems to produce some very major effects."

To make a fairly long story short, Mike agreed to take the antianxiety medication that I recommended, and its effects on his relationship with Shirley, whom I put on Anafranil, an antidepressant known to be effective for obsessive-compulsive disorder, were remarkable. He found himself more at peace with himself, and hence less apt to pick on Shirley. This, in turn, allowed Shirley to feel more relaxed and hence less compelled to seek the solace of "giving in" to her obsessive-compulsive habit. By succumbing to her compulsion, she had been avoiding the anxiousness that resisting her compulsion would produce. But now, with Mike's mellower attitude reducing her anxiety load overall, and with the help of the antiobsessional medication she was taking, she was better able to cope with that anxiousness. She had more strength because Mike was no longer such a drain. The two continue to take their medications to this day, though in reduced doses, and report that their lives are back to "normal" at last.

DRUGS TACKLE THE BIOLOGY

The story of Mike and Shirley illustrates a vital point: While environmental factors may be responsible for the way a depressive disorder develops, biological factors usually are responsible for the existence of the disorder in the first place. Mike's extreme irritability and Shirley's obsessive-compulsive disorder each grew worse because of the fused environment to which they were exposed, but their disorders were not "sired" by this environment. Biology did the siring. As we discussed in our "three shields" theory in Chapter 2, predispositions to depressive disorders usually are inherited at birth and then are either kindled or kept quiet depending on the circumstances of one's upbringing and adult life.

This is why I feel it's so important to treat depressive disorders from all possible angles. It's not enough to address just a depressed person's environment, behavior, patterns of thinking, or experiences from the past. His or her depressive *biology* also must be addressed. To miss this crucial element is like painting and waxing a car that's never been washed. The job just isn't going to last.

My approach to treating depression, therefore, is a multiple one: I use every available tool, because the problem can be so complex. I uncover as many causative factors as possible and I treat all of them—through specialized multimodal psychotherapies, through exercise and relaxation training, and, yes, through medication.

The development of highly effective and safe psychiatric medications in the past twenty years has been absolutely astounding. People who as little as thirty years ago might have had to spend their lives in institutions are now living more normal lives thanks to this amazing progress in understanding the human brain. It's a very encouraging and exciting time for those of us privy to the proper use of these literally lifesaving medicines.

Yet I must say that prescribing psychiatric medications is an art as well as a science—not all practitioners do it with the same level of expertise. This may seem scary on one level, but it also means that the right help is out there as long as you're willing to find it. We often get referrals at the Center for Mood Disorders from doctors and therapists whose patients have not responded to standard medication treatment and who need more specialized help. If this is true for you or your loved one, do not hesitate to contact your local medical center or psychiatric society to ask for the kind of specialist who can help you with your problem. An appointment with a psychopharmacologist is what you should request. And keep this in mind as you do: Even in cases where a depression is quite severe, medications used in conjunction with psychotherapy generally boast a success rate of between 75 and 85 percent. They can and do work.

What's Available and for What

Psychiatric medications are not the only method available for treating the biological element of depressive disorders. There's also electroconvulsive therapy (ECT) and light therapy. ECT is usually used as a last resort, however, because it can temporarily cause memory loss. Light therapy is generally restricted to treating Seasonal Affective Disorder (winter depression), a condition thought to be caused by the decreased amount of sunlight available during the winter.

This leaves medication treatment as the mainstay of biological therapy. Here's a brief rundown of what's currently available:

ANTIDEPRESSANT MEDICATIONS

I think it's important to understand that antidepressants do not lift one's mood falsely or briefly, as a street drug such as cocaine or "speed" might do. Antidepressants merely restore the functioning of the brain to normal. This restoration may feel like a boost to someone who's depressed, but trust me when I say it's no more artificial than insulin shots are for a diabetic. If a normal person were to take an antidepressant, there would be some side effects if anything at all, but no elevation of mood. This demonstrates that antidepressants merely "fix" what's in need of repair, rather than creating something artificial or unnatural.

There are many different kinds of antidepressants. The interesting thing about them is that no one medication has ever been shown to be more effective than any other in treating clinical depression, although individuals may respond better to one or two drugs while not to others. The art of using the medications is to try to find which drug will be best for a particular individual based on the kind of depression he has, his family history, and the side-effect profile of the particular medication.

The older class of antidepressants is called tricyclics and includes medications such as amitryptiline (Elavil), imipramine (Tofranil), nortriptyline (Pamelor, Aventyl), desipramine (Norpramin), protriptyline (Vivactil), and doxepin (Sinequan, Adapin). With the exception of desipramine and, to some extent, nortriptyline, these antidepressants are sedating and cause dry mouth and constipation quite frequently. They are all effective and reliable and have a good safety record, but are not highly effective against the more chronic and atypical forms of depression.

Newer medications, the heterocyclics, came along as the next generation of antidepressants. While they were no more or less effective than the tricyclics, they generally had fewer side effects, particularly for those patients who did not tolerate tricyclics well. Such antidepressants include trazadone (Desyrel), amoxapine (Asendin), and maprotiline (Ludiomil). Desyrel has become particularly popular because of its sleep-inducing and potent antianxiety properties, and because it is relatively benign in its effects on cardiac function. These characteristics, along with its high safety profile in the case of overdosage, has made it popular for use with the elderly, former drug abusers, and suicidal and medically ill patients.

The MAO inhibitors—Nardil, Marplan, and Parnate the most commonly known of the group—are very different kinds of antidepressants. Though they have been around for three decades, they fell out of favor because of their potential risks, which include life-threatening increases in blood pressure in those patients who mistakenly take certain contraindicated medications or eat fermented food products while taking one of these drugs.

The MAO inhibitors have become more widely used as psychiatrists, better trained in psychopharmacology and more confident in using these medications, have discovered that they are extremely effective in the treatment of atypical depression—depression characterized by high levels of anxiety, excessive sleep, and excessive appetite. They are also quite safe and effective for elderly patients. In addition to these depressive conditions, the MAO inhibitors are also extremely effective for panic disorder and the depressed phase of manic-depressive illness.

The final group of antidepressants might be called "novel agents," though within a few years, their names will be replaced by other, "more novel" medications. They are novel because they are structurally different than the other groups of antidepressants. These agents currently include fluoxetine (Prozac) and buproprion (Wellbutrin).

These medications represent significant advances in the medication treatment of depression, because they have relatively few side effects compared to other antidepressants. While they are equally effective in treating clinical depression as the other groups, Prozac in particular seems to be superior in treating atypical depression and chronic depression. It is also extremely effective for treating obsessive-compulsive disorder and depression associated with eating disorders.

Wellbutrin shows promise in treating people with depression associated with cocaine abuse, as well as those who have depression associated with attention-deficit disorder that has persisted from childhood. It may also be effective in the treatment of chronic-fatigue syndrome. As you can see, these "novel" antidepressant medications have been a major breakthrough in the pharmacologic treatment of depression.

Some other medications deserve special mention. Clomipramine (Anafranil), a tricyclic relative of imipramine, has recently been released in the United States for treatment of obsessive-compulsive disorder. It is a tricyclic antidepressant and therefore also effective for depression. Along with Prozac, it has revolutionized the treatment of people like Shirley.

Finally, Lithium, a naturally occurring salt, has been the mainstay of treatment for manic-depressive illness. It controls the manias and prevents the depressions. We now also use Lithium as an adjunctive treatment in clinical depression to "boost" the effectiveness of other antidepressants when a patient is not responding to conventional therapy. The combination of Lithium and specific antidepressants that are capable of being "boosted" may be the most potent medication treatment of depression currently available today. Recently, two medications that were used for years to treat seizures have been found to be effective for manic-depressive illness. Valproic acid (Depakote) and carbamazepine (Tegretol) were "accidentally" discovered to be very effective for many patients who did not respond to Lithium or who could not tolerate Lithium's side effects.

ANTIANXIETY MEDICATION

Anxiety may seem like the opposite of depression, but it's not. It is aligned very closely with depression, in fact, because it often causes the constant and uncontrollable worry on which many depressions are built. At the same time, depression can give birth to rather severe anxiety. So depression and anxiety are often intertwined with each other, much like the "chicken and the egg" relationship.

Controlling anxiety, therefore, becomes an important part of controlling depression, and this holds especially true for those who must live with someone who's depressed. Shirley's husband, Mike, as you'll recall, was suffering from an anxiety problem being made worse by his wife's obsessive-compulsive disorder. His anxiety, in turn, was further aggravating his wife's condition, so treating Mike's anxiety was an important first step in correcting their fused situation. I use antianxiety medications quite frequently to calm the anger-arousal levels of the loved ones of my depressed patients, especially during the all-important defusion process. Once defusion has been achieved, the medications can be reduced or eliminated entirely. Some common and very effective antianxiety medications are:

▲ Benzodiazepines—These are the well-known tranquilizer medications that include Xanax, Ativan, Valium, and Klonopin. Xanax and Klonopin, and to some extent Ativan, are effective for panic attacks, though only Xanax is FDA-approved for such use. These medications have received a great deal of media attention—both positive and negative. They are safe, effective medications, but must be managed by a skilled professional. Never regulate your own dose, never stop them abruptly, and stay away from them if you have a history of substance abuse.

They can be habit forming, but the risk of pathological addiction is very low if they are used properly. Some people do need to use them long-term. In these cases, treatment should always include regular follow-up and use of psychological antianxiety techniques such as hypnosis, meditation, relaxation training, and physical exercise, so that maintenance is continued at the lowest dose possible.

▲ Buspirone—This is one member of a new class of antianxiety medication that is marketed under the name Buspar and works quite differently from the benzodiazepines. The advantages of buspirone are that it is nonsedating, nonhabit-forming, and has antidepressant properties. The disadvantage is that it does not appear to be as effective as the benzodiazepines for reducing anxiety and does not work unless taken regularly for over a week. I have found it helpful for many patients with arousal problems, particularly in cases where benzodiazepines are poorly tolerated or abuse potential is high.

▲ Antidepressants—Antidepressants are also excellent for the management of anxiety and/or panic disorder. I frequently mix them with buspar or benzodiazepines for treating chronic anxiety. The newer antidepressants such as Prozac or some of the old reliable tricyclic antidepressants can be very effective for anxiety at lower doses than are required to treat depression.

Prevention

I wish I could tell you that depression was like the measles or mumps in that once gone, gone for good. But depression can recur even under professional treatment, and if untreated its chances of returning can run almost as high as 90 percent.

What this means is that you must be prepared, because how you react to these recurrences can be very influential in how severe they will be. Handled properly, they can be kept minor and brief, but allow yourself to overreact and fall back into your old patterns of fusion, and you could have a full-blown relapse on your hands. That being the case, please keep these three key prevention strategies in mind in the months, and even years, following your loved one's recovery.

1. *Stay cool, but also warm.* You mustn't panic in the event of a recurrence of your partner's depressed moods, but rather be compassionate and calm. Look for the kinds of negative self-perceptions and thoughts about life that may have characterized your partner's depression initially, and gently explain how they're invalid and are nothing more than recurrences of the "cognitive distortions" that depression can breed. Calmly remind your partner that giving in to such distortions can breed more depression.

Whatever you do, don't make the mistake of reacting to your partner's setback angrily or personally, as you may have reacted to his depression the first time. It's the same problem, which must be handled with the same empathy if it's going to remit. Research shows that the presence of a warm, caring, supportive, partner is the *single most important* psychological prevention against depression. So never downplay the value of having a good relationship with your depressed loved one.

2. *Keep in touch with your partner's therapist.* I generally encourage my patients to see me once a month for a year after they're over their depressions, and at least once every two to four months after that, for a kind of "checkup." I suggest you encourage your loved one to keep in contact with his or her therapist on a similar schedule, and I especially encourage you to have him see his therapist in the event of an apparent relapse. The faster a reemerging depression is treated, the easier it will be to bring back under control, and the less suffering it will cause for each of you.

3. *Encourage medication compliance.* Most major depressions have a life span of six to twelve months, so medications are generally prescribed for at least that long. It will be important for you to realize this because your loved one may suddenly feel "well" and want to toss his medication to the wind. To do so could be a serious mistake, so be watchful for such a scenario and don't be afraid to call your partner's therapist and ask for a joint session should it occur. Your loved one's depression also may be of a type that requires medication indefinitely, in which case medication compliance may need to be a lifetime affair. It's important for each of you in such a case not to view your loved one's medication as a "crutch," but rather as a necessary biological remedy for a very real biological problem.

Next on the agenda: dealing with "life after fusion." It's not always what people expect.

Coming Out
a Winner

7

VICTORY THROUGH COMPROMISE

"We live not as we wish, but as we can."

MENANDER 342–292 B.C.

"He's better, Doctor, much better, so please don't get me wrong. He hasn't had a drink or used any drugs in over six months and we don't fight anymore. But is this it? Is this as good as it's going to get? He still doesn't want to come to bed when I do, and he still likes to spend so much time alone. You've cured him, I guess, but you haven't cured our marriage."

Those were the words of Paul's wife, Karen, roughly a year after I started treating Paul, and her situation was an all-too familiar one. Paul's depression had lifted, but it hadn't revealed the charming or passionate prince Karen had been hoping for. What emerged instead was simply the real Paul, a kind and gentle man, but a very introspective one, someone less com-

159

fortable with people and conversation than with his own thoughts, a man who probably would never be able to give Karen the life-style or close emotional companionship she so desperately wanted. What was she to do?

I mention Karen's dilemma because it's one that you, too, could be facing in the months ahead, as the fusion-breaking strategies we've been discussing begin to have their effect. When the fighting stops, will you be satisfied with the quality of the peace? And as your partner's depression lifts, will you be happy with the person who emerges from behind it?

These are the difficult questions we'll be addressing in this chapter. We'll be looking at what I call the period of "reconstruction" that must follow the successful resolution of fusion, and yes, it's in many ways similar to the period of Reconstruction that took place following the Civil War. Just because the war is ended between you and your partner doesn't mean more work won't be needed to arrive at an acceptable truce. The resolution of the fusion and the lifting of your partner's depression will force each of you to confront who you really are, and what you really want from your relationship. There'll be no more hiding behind the fire and brimstone of combat. It will be time to see if "a more perfect union" can be achieved. And yes, some compromises may have to be made.

But you're tired of compromising, you say? Your life with your partner has been nothing but one huge compromise already, and you were hoping things could be better once he got well?

Things will be better. All I'm saying is that they may not be ideal. Just because your partner's mood becomes normal doesn't mean he's going to become wonderful. He's simply going to become the person he really is. This may come as a disappointment, as the real Paul came as a disappointment to Karen, but this is the reality you're going to have to be prepared to accept. By undergoing treatment that successfully restores his emotional health, your partner will be doing all that can be expected. If that's not enough, the next step is going to have to be up to you. You're either going to have to make the best of your situation, or you're going to have to leave it. Any other course will leave you feeling permanently miserable and short-changed.

When I told this to Karen, she accused me of kicking her when she was already down. "Are you telling me I'm somehow wrong for wanting to be with someone who can show me compassion and love?" she asked.

"You are if those desires are causing you to be unhappy," was my reply. "Your first responsibility to yourself should be your own well-being, not feeling that you have to live up to some idealized vision of what you think happiness should be."

Beware of Happiness, "Hollywood Style"

And with that, I launched into my speech about why so many of us today come up short in our happiness quests. We allow our standards for happiness to come not so much from our own realistic, self-generated visions as from fantasies of what we believe make others happy. This can be dangerous enough as we pursue the careers, cars, houses, and even phy-siques we see others enjoying, but it can be especially ill-fated as we pursue relationships. We want the ideal relationships we see being projected on television, or in the movies, or that we read about in books. Little do we realize that such relationships are less fact than fiction, and that few people actually enjoy lives that are so rosy.

Family influences also can sway our visions of happiness. We want our relationships to be as good as those our parents had, or, particularly if what they had was bad, we want far better. And we have become intolerant of disappointment and frustration of our expectations.

The end result, unfortunately, is that we wind up striving for goals that are more idealistic than realistic, goals that not only fail to take into adequate consideration the circumstances that really exist in our lives but that may not even reflect what we really are capable of delivering ourselves. It's human nature to want what we can't have. This is particularly true when it comes to the desire for closeness and caring from others. This leaves us like the cat chasing its tail as we pursue not only what may be out of reach, but what may not even be worth "catching" in the first place.

I call this discrepancy between the life you strive for and the life you are actually living your "misery gap". The wider it is, the less happiness you're going to have.

When I explained my "misery gap" concept to Karen, she responded predictably. She wanted to know—as I'm sure you do, too—how the gap might be narrowed.

I had several suggestions, but I started by recommending we make sure she really wanted what she *thought* she wanted in the first place. Outside influences, remember, sometimes can have us searching for relationships that might not even be right for us to find.

And sure enough, Karen said she was hoping to avoid the fate of her parents, who had divorced after fifteen turbulent years when she was only ten. "I was hoping my marriage could be different—safer, warmer, and more loving."

Yet, when I proceeded to ask Karen about other relationships she had experienced, she had to confess that she had felt "suffocated" by more than a few overly attentive boyfriends in both high school and college. "I guess that's why I liked Paul," she said. "He was aloof, and I found him mysterious and challenging."

"But you don't any longer?" I had to ask.

"It's different now. We've been married for fifteen years, and those kinds of games should be over."

I could tell Karen knew she was on thin ice, but I wasn't going to save her. "Now that Paul's not depressed anymore, how does he compare to the man you married?" I asked.

"He's pretty much the same, I guess."

"And yet you're faulting him now for being distant?"

"People should grow closer together when they're married,

but that hasn't happened with us. We seem to be getting farther apart."

By questioning Karen further, I learned what I suspected. She had allowed herself to become totally dependent on Paul—financially as well as emotionally—so that his aloofness now loomed not as a turn-on but a threat. Adding irony to her injury was that Karen didn't really even *want* the doting kind of husband she thought she did. She was merely reacting to the idealized image of marriage she thought would protect her from the fate of her parents.

When I explained this to Karen, she bristled, and understandably so. I told her that by reacting to what she thought her marriage *should* be, she was missing the chance to enjoy it for what it *could* be. Paul had done all he could do by going for treatment and stabilizing his substance abuse and mood disturbance. The next move would have to be up to her. She was going to have to narrow her "misery gap" by bringing her demands of Paul more in line with what he realistically could be expected to give. Paul wasn't going to be able to change much more—I warned her of that.

But Karen *would* be able to change. She could reduce her feelings of emptiness and change her belief that greater caring and intimacy with Paul were the only solutions to her despair. These changes would require fortifying herself in other ways and interacting more closely with family members and friends. "You have all your eggs in your husband's basket right now," I told her. "No wonder you want him to hold you so close."

Karen took my advice. She pursued outside interests and made efforts to be closer to family members and friends. This gradually allowed her to reduce her demands on Paul, which in turn made him more willing to give.

We'll be returning to Karen and Paul in Chapter 8, because their story is a truly inspiring one, but let's stop here and look at what Karen learned:

She learned that her expectations for her relationship with Paul had come to be dictated more by her idealized visions and her own insecurities than by the factors that had attracted her to Paul in the first place.

She learned that this misguided perspective created a large discrepancy between the relationship she yearned for and the one she believed she had, thus creating a giant "misery gap" that would have to be narrowed if an acceptable level of happiness was going to return to their relationship.

So that's precisely what we did. We narrowed her misery gap—as you can narrow yours—by shrinking it from both ends. We made adjustments in both her ideal world and her real world so that such an untenable discrepancy no longer existed between the two. She adjusted her ideal world by lowering her expectations of what Paul would be able to deliver—she began setting *achievable* goals for the relationship. She then modified her real-world emotional experiences by raising her opinions and expectations of herself. The better she could feel about herself based on her own actions, the less she would need to rely on actions from Paul.

Look for the Good, Not the Bad

What Karen learned is what you, too, must learn: Making peace with your partner requires making peace with yourself. This is important for stopping fusion, as we saw in Chapter 4, but it's just as important once fusion is over. Fusion will return, and your partner's depression could return, if you allow disappointment with your situation to rekindle your old argumentative ways. This doesn't mean accepting the progress of your partner's rehabilitation unconditionally, but it does mean being understanding and realistic. Full remission of your partner's depressed behavior may take longer than the period during which he's under actual treatment, so be patient. Also, be willing to switch doctors if recovery appears stalled. What you mustn't do is show frustration or despair over your partner's progress. We now know, based on our understanding of how fusion contributes to depression, that when you harshly criticize or chastise your partner for setbacks, such negativity can spread to him and could reignite his depression.

The attitude you must have during and after the months of your loved one's recovery is one of optimism. Look for the positive changes that are occurring in your partner, not sticking points or relapses. This may be difficult at times as you begin to fear a return of his depression, but you'll only be inviting that return by showing such fear. You must remain calm and show confidence, so that your partner will not fuse with your anxieties. By showing anger or fear, you'll only be eroding the chances for continuing recovery and prevention of future recurrences.

I recently had occasion to tell this to Tom's wife, Marsha, whom we met in Chapter 1. While she agreed with me in principle, she confessed she would have trouble implementing my advice in the flesh. "He can still be so haughty and obstinate, especially if he's been drinking. He doesn't go into his tirades anymore, and he's definitely much better with the kids, but he still can be cold and harsh with me. Down deep I think he just has very little respect for women, and it infuriates me."

Marsha went on for twenty minutes complaining of Tom's "macho-mania," his vanity, and his aggravating need to "strut around like J. R. Ewing himself."

When she had finally finished, I asked her if she thought she had told me anything that either of us didn't already know. And of course, she hadn't. She had merely expressed her anger and disappointment at who her husband was, at how treatment was smoothing his rough edges but failing to shape somebody new—someone she would like to have as a husband.

"Can't you tell me anything more that's been positive about Tom since he's been in treatment?" I asked.

She took a deep breath, stared at the ceiling for a moment, and spoke more calmly.

"He's more willing to listen to me now when I need to express my feelings, that's been good. And he's more helpful around the house. And he doesn't drink during the day anymore like he used to."

"Anything else?"

"I think he's somewhat more open about his own feelings. We can have some good heart-to-heart discussions now that we couldn't have before."

"Those are some pretty substantive changes," I told her. "And they're very important ones because they're the kind that can serve as the foundation for more improvements in the future. The two of you are communicating now in a way that you weren't able to before, and that's a very good sign. You've got to nurture that communication, not destroy it by falling back into fusion. Tom is making significant progress, and though I doubt he'll ever become the companion of your dreams, he's at least moving in the right direction. Don't block him by expecting too much too fast."

Your Negotiable vs. Nonnegotiable Needs

But I didn't stop there with Marsha. I told her that if she honestly felt Tom was not going to be able to become an acceptable partner for her, she would have to muster the courage to leave him. She was doing no one any good by continuing to play the role of a victim. Did she want in or did she want out? If she wanted in, she would have to stop complaining and start working with Tom, rather than against him. And if she wanted out, she'd have to be able to tell him why and then take action. By making no decision, she was making a wrong decision because she was perpetuating despair—both hers and Tom's—risking a recurrence of fusion, and hence of Tom's depression.

"But there's so much to consider, so many pros and cons. Either decision—staying or leaving—seems like a bad one," she said.

If you can identify with Marsha's dilemma, you have my sympathy. The proposition of ending a long-standing relationship, no matter how bad it's been, is never a comfortable one. You have so much of yourself invested in the relationship, so many experiences and memories, that to leave it will feel like giving up part of yourself.

It's a sacrifice you may have to make, however, if there can be no growth for you in your partner's presence. Growth is a key issue here. If you cannot move forward in the direction of the person you want to be, if you cannot pursue your realistic visions of what you would like your life to become, then your relationship should be ended. Every person has a set of non-negotiable needs that must be met in a relationship, and if the needs cannot be met, the relationship should not be endured.

If I sound firm about that, it's because I am. Emotional health, like physical health, requires certain "essential nutrients" to remain strong. Without these essential nutrients, emotional health can weaken, and despair grows high.

These essential emotional nutrients can be divided into two basic categories: those that nurture security and those that nurture self-esteem.

SECURITY

Security is important in a relationship because it provides the very fundamental and vital feeling of safety. Without it, anxiety can build, which can be quite unhealthy for some people, especially those who may have experienced insecure childhoods. The lack of security they feel with their partners reawakens their fears from the past.

If this is true in your relationship—and I'm talking about financial and physical security as well as emotional security—then one of your essential emotional needs, one of your "non-negotiables," is being violated, and changes need to be made. Some of the changes may be able to come from you—the pursuit of a more substantial income, for example, if financial security is the issue—but many will be up to your loved one. If your partner is guilty of any of the following security "violations" on a consistent basis, and you see no signs of improvement in these areas even once professional treatment is under way, then your case for leaving must be considered that much more valid for each infraction incurred.

IMPERMISSIBLE VIOLATIONS OF SECURITY

▲ Your partner makes repeated threats of separation or divorce.

▲ Your partner flirts in your presence and seems to enjoy making you feel jealous and unsafe in the relationship.

▲ Your partner has sexual encounters or affairs with others.

▲ Your partner goes places or does things he or she keeps secret.

▲ Your partner is chronically hostile to you, either directly or passively.

▲ Your partner makes you feel financially insecure by unilaterally controlling family finances and expenditures.

▲ Your partner makes no attempts whatsoever to be supportive, even when you ask for help.

▲ Your partner insists on dominating you.

▲ Your partner shows you no interest sexually and has no desire for sexual contact with you.

Remember that these are not necessarily reasons to consider ending your relationship. Some of these issues may not even be true "nonnegotiable" emotional needs for you to feel safe in a relationship. If they are, and if your partner is working toward improving in these areas, you should be patient and hope for the best. But if progress is not being made, or your partner is refusing even to try to improve in these areas, then you have every right to call it quits.

SELF-ESTEEM

Just as important as feeling secure in a relationship is feeling worthwhile. If you're involved with someone who's constantly undermining your self-esteem, you're being violated as much as if you were being subjected to physical abuse. And here again, if you have problems with self-esteem that stem from your childhood, any later attacks on your self-esteem are going to hurt that much more. The best relationships are those that boost self-esteem, and while it may not be possible for your partner to do that for you in the initial stages of his recovery, it could be forthcoming, so stay hopeful. Your concern at this point should simply be that you not allow your self-esteem to be attacked. Here are key affronts to look for.

IMPERMISSIBLE ATTACKS ON SELF-ESTEEM

▲ Your partner attempts to make you feel unattractive or sexually undesirable through degrading remarks or actions.
▲ Your partner makes repeated attacks on your intelligence.
▲ Your partner repeatedly questions your honesty or morals.
▲ Your partner enjoys criticizing you in public.
▲ Your partner degrades your worthiness as a parent and blames the children's problems on you alone.
▲ Your partner treats you as if you can't be trusted.
▲ Your partner chronically accuses you of lacking ambition or of not having worthwhile goals or meaningfulness in life.

Please remember again, however, that in the aftermath of fusion, some "heat" may remain, and your partner may be guilty of some of the above violations out of sheer momentum. Be patient. Continue to set limits and to manage your relationship according to the guidelines we set in Chapter 5. But don't be masochistic. If these behaviors continue for more than several months after fusion has stopped, you may be dealing with a lost cause. Your own emotional well-being is your first responsibility, remember. Neither you nor your partner will have anything to gain by your continued abuse.

GETTING BY GIVING

Security and self-esteem: they're your nonnegotiables. Without them, there can be no stable future for your relationship, so if you can see no hope of obtaining them, you should strongly consider getting out.

But as we saw with Karen, it's sometimes possible to obtain these essential needs by making changes not in your partner, but in yourself. This is an important aspect of any compromise process—getting by giving—and it applies to personal relationships, especially.

In Karen's case, she worked to bolster her sense of security and her self-esteem by pursuing outside interests and achieving greater intimacy with family and friends. This allowed her to be more accepting of Paul's inability to provide her with these nonnegotiables as a husband. Paul was not holding out on these essential emotional needs intentionally—that's a key issue. It simply was not within his emotional makeup to be able to provide Karen with these essentials to the degree she seemed to need. This is an important point, one which you must keep in mind as you begin to enter into the compromise process yourself. You must weigh your partner's ability to give against your own ability to get. If you're demanding that your partner go against his nature to provide what you might actually be *better equipped* to obtain on your own, your demands at the bargaining table are not in the best of faith.

Karen was able to become a much happier and more complete person by realizing that she could not count on Paul for her entire gamut of emotional needs. She learned to see him as just one contributor—a major contributor, but not the only contributor—to the emotional sustenance she needed to be happy and well.

Tom's wife, Marsha, by contrast, seemed less willing to

provide for herself in this regard. She had more trouble than Karen in accepting her husband for who he was—partially because Tom's recovery had been less complete than Paul's, but also because of her own reluctance to face reality. That reluctance, I soon learned, stemmed from emotional scars she still bore from her childhood. Her father had abandoned the family when she was 13, and somehow she expected Tom to fill that void. Her unhappy childhood also had failed to instill her with the strength and confidence that becoming independent of Tom would require. She felt "trapped," and her resentment showed in her angry insistence that Tom be an emotional as well as a financial provider of the highest order.

My point here is simply this: You can improve your chances of arriving at an acceptable compromise with your loved one if you assume more responsibility for obtaining your nonnegotiable needs for yourself. This doesn't mean letting your partner off the hook totally, but it does mean shouldering what you can. Knowing that your efforts will be for your benefit—regardless of whether your relationship works out or not—should be all the incentive you need. Yes, wounds you may have suffered during your upbringing could make such efforts seem difficult at first, but know that these efforts will help heal those wounds. As we'll be exploring in greater detail in our next chapter, coming to grips with the aftermath of fusion can provide opportunities for growth that can be highly beneficial for all concerned.

When Things Go Badly—When to Call it Quits

But I'd be lying to say things always work out. Sometimes a depression cannot be cured (true in 5 to 10 percent of all cases). It's also possible that your partner's degree of recovery could turn out to be unacceptable to you, no matter how understanding you try to be. Then, too, your partner could refuse even to go for help. The number of emotionally disturbed people currently refusing to receive treatment is quite staggering—they outnumber treated patients by roughly two to one, in fact—so don't be shocked if your loved one falls into this category. Approximately 20 percent of all Americans suffer from a diagnosable emotional disorder of some type, yet only 30 to 35 percent of them are receiving help. This means that twenty-eight million of us—roughly one in ten—has an emotional problem on the loose. The statistic does not speak highly of the degree to which we've accepted emotional disorders as legitimate medical concerns.

THE DECISION TREE

So what do you do if your loved one's depression, for whatever reason, shows no signs of going away?

You've got to be absolutely certain, first of all, that you've been doing everything possible to defuse. If you still have any doubts about what this involves, please look back at Chapters 4 and 5. No decision you make can be the right decision if you're still in a fused state with your partner, because neither of you will be seeing your situation for what it really is. You *must* clear the smoke of fusion before you can assess the true severity of what you face.

Once you have defused, however, here's what to look for. You should strongly consider ending your relationship if:

1. Your partner continues to act in the ways that promoted the fusion between you in the first place. You see virtually no improvement, in other words, or even attempts at improvement of the conditions you find so upsetting. Even worse, you hear repeated denial by your loved one that he is contributing in any way to problems in the relationship.

2. You honestly feel that to continue the relationship would mean living with fusion indefinitely, or that so much effort would be required to combat the fusion that you'd have little energy for anything else.

3. Your visions and goals for both the present and the future are so fundamentally different from your partner's that no unified plan could ever seem possible.

4. Each of you has exhausted all avenues of outside help for dealing with your differences. In your loved one's case, if his depression persists, I would ask that he has tried at least two skilled professionals specially trained in dealing with depressions that are "treatment resistant."

DIFFERENT WAYS TO LEAVE YOUR LOVER

Paul Simon sang of fifty ways, but I can guarantee you he employed considerable poetic license in arriving at that figure. In my many years of observing couples attempting to separate in ways short of permanent and legally binding divorce, I've seen only two ways that produced reasonably consistent stability and overall improvement in their relationship. One of the ways is what I call "therapeutic separation," which we examined in Chapter 6. You separate under the supervision of a therapist for a designated period with the express purpose of working your differences out.

But another way is what I call "separation under one roof." This method allows you to live essentially separate lives, but without legally terminating your marital contract. It can be risky, because there's always the chance that fusion will be rekindled, and it has the distinct disadvantage of limiting the intimacy that can be achieved with new people, because you are still married and living in the same house. But for some couples it can work. The case of Andrea and Randy might help you decide if it can work for you.

SEPARATION UNDER ONE ROOF: ANDREA AND RANDY

Andrea is a women in her mid 50s who had experienced several major depressions in her life, one of which caused her to be hospitalized for several weeks. She continued to suffer from recurrences of her depression throughout her marriage, becoming harsh and distant with each episode. Her husband, Randy, was always a prime target for her misery, anger, and resentment. Randy would respond by taking Andrea's behavior personally, which would cause him to fuse with her. He'd react to her irritability and lack of sexual desire as evidence that she was a "man hater" interested only in herself. This in turn would cause Andrea to view Randy as insensitive as well as insecure, and fusion eruptions would be almost daily affairs.

They tried therapy with me—both individually and jointly—but couldn't seem to stop the fusion. They continued to focus on each other, and neither of them ever took personal responsibility for contributing to the fusion. They would not unlock from the reactive mode that fusion creates, and forever blamed *each other* for their harsh or critical reactions. Randy was fed up with constantly feeling "rejected" by Andrea's sexual apathy, and he decided he wanted out. Andrea agreed that divorce was the best solution, but when it came down to who was actually going to pack his or her bags, neither would step forward. They went on this way for weeks—each agreeing that divorce was inevitable, but neither willing to make the first move.

Eventually the reason for the stalemate became clear to me. While the romance between them was gone, there still was a very fundamental bond. They had spent more than half their lives together and raised four children, and they were having trouble giving that much of themselves up. Neither had the courage or the will to start totally anew.

The fusion between them persisted despite this bond, however, so gradually Randy started staying out late during the week and spending weekends away from home entirely. This angered Andrea initially, but in time she started developing interests and friendships outside of their relationship as well. They continued to share the house, and would always be sure to get together for family occasions and holidays, and on rare occasions would even get together for sex. Other than that, however, they lived separate lives, which they did not share or discuss with each other. Sadly, this was the only way they could defuse.

A strange relationship, to be sure, but it worked for them. It's been ten years since they started living this way and each has told me that they've never been happier, though they acknowledge the imperfections of their situation. I always ask if they're ready for a "real divorce" or a "remarriage" when I see them, but no. In many ways each has the best of both worlds, they tell me. They've avoided the financial and emotional traumas of divorce, yet they enjoy many of the freedoms of a single life. Most importantly, they've stopped the fusion between them, and Andrea's emotional health is much improved. She has not had a recurrence of depression since they began this new living arrangement—a testimony to the antidepressant power of defusing.

I have since had other couples do as Andrea and Randy did, and with similarly positive results. Some couples have eventually reunited, while others have continued to live in this separation-under-one-roof relationship. Separation under one roof is most suited for people who are not independent enough to strike out into the world on their own, and in this sense can be a worthwhile compromise and highly effective alternative to the usually traumatic experience of divorce. Whether or not it's right for you, however, only you can say.

If divorce seems just too "drastic"—financially as well as emotionally—pulling apart as Andrea and Randy did could be an appropriate interim move, if not necessarily an ultimate solution. Do be careful if young children are involved, however, as you want to do everything possible to maintain a secure and peaceful environment for them. The "emotional divorce" of the separation-under-one-roof solution is less than ideal when children are still living in the house, though it is clearly a better alternative than living in a chronically fused, chaotic family environment.

THE "REAL THING" CAN BE THE RIGHT THING: DAVID AND KATHY

Let me say first that divorce should not be considered until all other options have been explored. This means that you have done everything possible to defuse from your partner, and that he or she either has refused to receive treatment or the treatment has failed. This leaves you with the "no-win" situation of having constantly to be on guard against fusion flare-ups as well as having to struggle daily to maintain a positive and healthy self-image. Such a situation may exceed your capacity to cope, and hence be an unacceptable violation of your right to live a happy and well-adjusted life. It's a burden you should not have to bear. Every person has an inalienable right to feel safe, needed, and worthy, and if your current relationship is violating that right, it should be ended. There is nothing noble about bearing pain for no other reasons than guilt, fear, and misplaced obligation—especially when no one is gaining from it.

As frightening as the prospect of divorce can be, you must understand that it can be far more of a beginning for you than an end. By coming to the decision that divorce is your only remaining option, you will have learned things about yourself that you could have learned in no other way. Your real goals, your real needs, your real fears—*the real you*—all will become invaluably clear to you as you gather the information you will need in deciding to bring your relationship to an end. We'll be talking more about this in our next chapter, but I mention it now so that you can view your prospects for divorce in the proper light. It can be the start of the best part of your life.

Unfortunately, so many couples divorce unnecessarily—as a desperate attempt to escape the fusion they neither understand nor know how to counteract. The case of David and Kathy comes to mind as a fitting example of a couple who divorced at the right time and for the right reasons. David, 44, had been under treatment by a psychotherapist for a period of eight years when he came to see me. He was seeing no improvement whatsoever, and he and Kathy were tightly fused. Kathy felt rejected because of David's inability to interact with her—sexually as well as emotionally—and she also was experiencing extreme anxiety over his frequent and secretive gambling sprees. David, on the other hand, viewed Kathy as domineering, manipulative, overly critical—"an insane worrier" who was virtually impossible to please.

I started David on Prozac, a new antidepressant that had just come on the market, and the results were quite dramatic. He had more energy, his sense of humor returned, he was better able to concentrate, and he no longer felt overwhelmed by pessimism and self-doubt.

These improvements did not translate into an improvement in his relationship with Kathy, however. On the contrary, things actually got worse as many of the behaviors that bothered Kathy simply gained new energy. He continued to gamble with the family savings and lie about it, and his renewed self-confidence inspired him to take on business deals that gave him even less time to be with Kathy or the kids. The lifting of David's depression had revealed someone that Kathy clearly did not like.

I started seeing Kathy individually, and learned very quickly that she had developed a drinking problem in her attempts to cope. She was numbing herself to the reality of her situation rather than confronting it, and I told her there could be no improvement until she could stand up and face life without her alcoholic crutch. She resisted at first, but finally agreed to join AA and experienced a near epiphany. Through sober eyes, she could see that she had been avoiding truths about herself and truths about David. She had no clear vision of herself outside of her fused relationship with her husband, and she had been using alcohol to sedate herself to the reality that David probably was never even going to come close to being a stable companion. His recent recovery had been a traumatic disappointment for her, "like finding that the pot at the end of the rainbow is filled with coal," she told me.

We agreed that an all-out self-improvement plan could be

her only escape. She resumed her job as a hairdresser, started exercising regularly, and changed her dietary habits so that she was no longer eating out of self-pity. Gradually her self-confidence grew, she felt desirable and self-sufficient—she was ready to tell David he had better shape up or ship out. She now finally had a realistic vision of what life could be without him, and she was ready to pursue it by herself, or with someone else, if he was not willing to comply with her needs.

She confronted David one evening over dinner, and his reaction was predictable though disappointing. Kathy told him she was willing to be patient and go to joint treatment with him, but that he at least would have to acknowledge he still had some problems and be willing to work on them.

"But he said that he was fully cured, and that he had never had a gambling problem in the first place," she told me. "He said I was just being my usual meddling and worrisome self. And when I told him that I needed at least some sexual contact with him, he said that would be impossible as long as I insisted on 'emasculating' him. In the old days that would have made me furious. But this time it just made me realize what I had to do."

I told Kathy that I had great respect for what she had done. Rationally and calmly—but firmly—she had made a stand for her "nonnegotiable" needs, and when David refused to comply, she had the courage to accept that there would have to be a change. Her essential needs for self-esteem and security were not going to be met, and while that saddened her, she no longer was going to let it paralyze her. She calmly informed David that he had twenty-four hours to reconsider his position. Yes, he was to be commended for seeking help for his depression, but his gambling with the family savings and insensitivity to her most vital needs still remained issues of great concern to her. If he was not willing to seek help in these areas, and if he was not going to be able to share in her vision of what a happy life between them could be, then she deserved the chance to start anew.

The next morning over breakfast, David made the mistake of calling what he thought was Kathy's bluff. He essentially told her that she'd have to get out of the kitchen if she didn't like the smell of the soup.

So that's precisely what she did. She moved to her own apartment with their two children within a month, and got divorce proceedings under way soon after that.

Should we think of this ending between Kathy and David as a bad one?

I don't think so. Divorce is never without pain and deep feelings of loss, but it also can be the opportunity for great gains. Kathy went on to remarry a very sensitive and loving man, and eventually opened her own shop. She looks back on her years with David as unfortunate, but also valuable, in that they forced her into the kind of self-examination she needed to realize who she really wanted to be. Even David gained from the experience, although painfully. He wound up in bankruptcy as his gambling problem finally got the best of him, but joined Gambler's Anonymous as a result. He has not remarried and says he probably never will. "Some of us just weren't cut out for it," he now has the insight and honesty to admit. I hope he will be able to change his perspective of marriage and intimate relationships with women as his recovery continues.

SEPARATING FROM A FAMILY MEMBER

Terminating a dysfunctional marriage, once you've made the decision to do it, is a relatively easy procedure, with certainly no shortage of laws or lawyers to help you.

But what if the relationship that has become dysfunctional is with one of your parents, one or more of your children, or brother, sister, grandparent, uncle or aunt, or a close friend? You can't file for a divorce from one of them.

True, but you can implement an effective separation, nonetheless. You can disengage emotionally as well as physically, and you *must* if you feel your nonnegotiable needs are being violated. We saw this to a moderate degree with Josie, in Chapter 5, who learned to distance herself from her parents in order to protect her self-esteem. However, an even greater distance may be required in cases where violations of nonnegotiable needs are more severe. The case of Lesley and her father, Joshua, is a good example.

Joshua was suffering from a depression caused in large part by the death of his wife, Margaret, to whom he had been married for forty-three years. Lesley invited her father to live with her and her family, thinking it would help him through his depression, but it didn't seem to help. Joshua would start drinking every afternoon at precisely four o'clock and be stumbling drunk by eight. Lesley found it upsetting, but she was even more concerned about the effects her father's behavior was having on her children and her marriage. Her husband wanted Joshua to be set up in his own apartment, but Lesley was worried that he would follow through with his threats of suicide if he were forced to live alone. She asked her father to seek professional help, but he refused. There'd be no "head doctor" for him. What was Lesley to do? Her father's condition did not qualify him for involuntary hospitalization under the law—he was not an active threat to himself or to others.

I advised her to strive for a compromise—set him up in his own apartment, but assure him he'd be welcome to visit at any time. However, there would be strict limits on his behavior: He would not be allowed inside her house if he was noticeably tipsy when he arrived, no alcohol at all was allowed inside her house, and there were to be no remorseful ruminations over the past or complaints of neglect by her or other family members.

The plan allowed Lesley to defend her nonnegotiable right to assure a positive environment for her and for her family. It also allowed her the emotional safety she needed so that she could feel motivated and comfortable in being supportive, caring, and compassionate. She told Joshua this, and he seemed to understand. He agreed to the compromise, and also eventually agreed to get help for his depression. Lesley's limit setting had forced him either to face his own problems constructively, and thereby receive support from the family, or to remain alone and depressed at home.

But what if the depressed person is one of your children?

This presents a more difficult situation, certainly, but not an impossible one. Your first goal should be to employ all the strategies we've talked about to defuse. This includes refusing to become highly emotional, learning to set limits on how your child may treat you, and understanding that an emotional illness—and not just a "bad kid"—is what you're up against.

Perhaps most important, however, is finding the right emotional distance from which to relate to a seriously depressed child. This may be difficult, as your natural parenting instinct will be to take control of the situation and dominate it. But as we have noted over and over again, the resulting fusion caused by such action would do more harm than good. You should make every effort possible to get your child to receive professional help, and in some extreme cases—those involving behavior that is violent or suicidal—hospitalization should strongly be considered.

Other cases, where hospitalization against the child's will is not possible, will require the strictest of limit setting and may include putting your child out of the house if his behavior becomes threatening or otherwise intolerable. Organizations such as Tough Love exist to help parents in such dire straits. I suggest using such community resources and the guidance of a child psychiatrist, whom you can visit even if your child refuses, to help clarify your options and coordinate care.

It's time now to see how learning to deal with a loved one's depression can provide a unique opportunity for emotional growth. This cloud does have a silver lining, after all.

SPIRALING UP—GAINING FROM THE PAIN

Ad astra per aspera ("To the stars through hardship").

LATIN PROVERB

I should say before starting this chapter that my reputation as a psychotherapist and a physician is one of being staunchly realistic. I consider overly optimistic promises to be bad business as well as bad science.

Realist that I am, however, I am also keenly aware that some of the darkest clouds can have the most silver linings. "Adversity doth best discover virtue," is how Francis Bacon put it, an observation that holds especially true regarding the hardship of having to live in close contact with a depressed person. This seeming misfortune can provide opportunities for self-discovery and emotional growth that might be experienced in no other way.

I call this process of self-discovery and emotional growth "spiraling up," and in many ways it is fusion in reverse. Whereas fusion erodes individuality and self-esteem, spiraling up nourishes these qualities. People who spiral up begin to feel more independent, more self-directed, more energetic, and more optimistic than they've ever felt in their lives. By freeing themselves from the negative forces of fusion, they're better able to generate positive forces from within themselves. And if their partners also are able to free themselves from fusion, a reinforcing effect can occur whereby couples spiral up together. Instead of infecting each other with hostility and despair, they begin infecting each other with empathy, hope, and love. The contagious-emotions phenomenon gets turned around so that the vicious cycle of depression becomes a propitious cycle of happiness.

As the realist again, however, I must tell you that spiraling up takes work, work that will be in addition to the defusion strategies we discussed in Chapters 4 and 5. Defusing will serve the important function of disengaging you from the destructive forces of fusion so that you can be free to rebuild yourself in the image of your choice—but what will that image be? How will it be different from the way you are now? What new goals will you have and how committed will you be to attaining these goals? What will you learn about yourself regarding why you fell prey to fusion in the first place, and what will you do to prevent it from ever happening again?

These are the kinds of questions you're going to have to ask yourself—and answer—if spiraling up is going to be possible. As I tell my patients, you can't spiral up until you've understood why you spiraled down. Self-improvement has to be based on self-knowledge, and self-knowledge can come only through self-examination. And from this self-examination must come a healthy new vision of yourself—a vision you must be motivated to achieve if your life is to change significantly for the better.

Defusion, therefore, is not the end of your happiness quest, but really only the beginning. You'll be stopping the war by defusing and bringing greater peace to your relationship, but you're still going to have to learn why the war started if you're going to achieve greater peace with yourself.

That being the case, let's back up for a moment. You may think your problems with your loved one have been rooted squarely in the present, but fusion is not that simple. It feasts on vulnerabilities born also from the past, "learned behaviors" that can come back to haunt you as fusion forces you back into ways of thinking and acting that you learned very early in life. Such role-playing not only tends to make fusion worse, it prevents the kind of emotional growth needed for a happy and well-adjusted adult life. Let's look at this phenomenon of role-playing more closely.

Why the Real You Hasn't Stood Up: The Conformity Trap

In every family, there are two fundamental yet opposing forces that determine the individuality of each of its members. One force nurtures self-esteem and encourages independence from the family structure. This is the force responsible for the kind of self-confidence and emotional strength it takes for us finally to leave the nest and function effectively in the outside world. In emotionally healthy families, this force is strong.

The second force is quite different, however. It's a force of conformity that discourages independence and invites family members to adopt roles within the family hierarchy that tend to stifle individuality and self-esteem. This force usually is strongest in families that are *not* emotionally healthy, where one or both parents may suffer from an emotional disorder, and where fusion is often present.

Which of the two forces predominates?

That depends on both the family and the person. If you come from a family in which one or both of your parents were emotionally disturbed, guilt provoking, or fearsome—and/or your basic personality structure is more passive and dependent than strong willed and independent—the force of conformity in you is going to be very strong. You're going to have low self-esteem, and your susceptibility to falling into unhealthy roles—especially when confronted by a depressed loved one—is going to be very great. Just the opposite will be true, or course, if your parents were well adjusted and/or your basic psychological makeup is a strong one.

But my guess is that many of you come from families that were plagued by much of the same fusion that you currently face in your life with your depressed loved one. Your self-esteem may be relatively low as a result, causing you to fall back into roles you learned to play as a child, roles unlikely to be appropriate for dealing effectively with the adverse conditions you presently face.

That might sound like a scolding, but it's not meant to. The highly impressionable years we spend as children often mark us in ways that are more indelible than we know. This puts us at risk of living our lives by imitating the past as much as by responding suitably to the present—a danger that's especially imminent in the face of fusion. Fusion causes you to act in ways that are "reactionary" rather than rational, ways that pull you back into old roles rather than encourage you to explore new ones. You get knocked down to your most basic level of emotional functioning when you're fused, and it causes you to embrace the behaviors that are most familiar to you—ones you may have used to protect yourself from other emotional crises you faced early in your life.

So am I telling you that your personality was molded years ago, and that your emotional heritage has branded you in ways that are impossible to change?

Absolutely not. I'm simply saying that fusion has put your emotional development in a time warp, that it has caused you to regress rather than progress, and that the time to move forward is now.

"But how?" you ask. "If my level of self-esteem started out low because of my upbringing, and it's been knocked down even further by the fusion I've been experiencing with my depressed partner, what chance do I have of building it up? Can a person really improve his self-concept?"

Patients invariably ask that when I explain fusion's effects, and my answer is always the same: "You can change if you have the determination and courage." I don't tell them they can expect a personality transplant, but I do tell them they can achieve a significant make-over and that the amount of improvement they can expect will be proportional to the amount of effort they're willing to invest. Spiraling up is not an epiphany, it's a gradual process of self-discovery based as much on accepting your limitations and the limitations of those closest to you as on maximizing your strengths. Just as you may need to make compromises in achieving peace with your "recovered" loved one, you may need to make compromises in achieving peace with yourself. People who are the happiest and best adjusted are not those who are perfect or the most idealistic, but rather realistic. They've learned to strive for what they *can have* rather than agonizing over what they can't—an important point to keep in mind as we explore my spiraling-up strategies, which lie ahead. No one is emotionally perfect or should ever expect to be. Such an expectation would be a sizable imperfection in itself. You must think of perfection simply as being the best you can be. And a good way to start is by acknowledging to what degree the phenomenon of role-playing and "role reliving" has thus far been directing your life.

Acknowledging the Roles You Play

What follows is a list of the roles I most frequently see fusion forcing people to play. If any hit home, please be appropriately alerted. If you're reverting to behaviors of the past, it's very unlikely that you're responding suitably to the present. You're going to have to unlearn your old behaviors and begin learning some new ones. I'm a firm believer that you can't make behavioral changes for the future until you've adequately understood the forces from your past that control your behavior in the present.

The Scapegoat/Victim Role: If you were frequently the object of unfair attacks as a child, you may have fallen into a similar role with your depressed partner. You get blamed for his or her bad moods, bad luck, bad job performances, or bad whatever, and you accept it. The acceptance has a price, however, as you feel resentment, whether you choose to express it or not. This fuses you with your depressed partner even more, and his unfair attacks continue with even more vigor as a result.

The Caretaker Role: Your position is one of a psychological nursemaid—again, a possible throwback to a similar role you may have played as a child. You feel responsible for your depressed partner's well-being, and your moods hinge on his moods accordingly. You're up when he's up and down when he's down—not a good situation for you or your relationship, as you eventually begin to resent this bondage. You also may find yourself being subjected to injustices and disrespect in your caretaker role, which can fuel fusion, injure your self-esteem, and coerce you into playing your caretaker role even more.

The Peacemaker Role: You're the National Guard, United Nations, and Red Cross combined. When tempers flare between your depressed partner and other family members, it's your job to step in and restore the peace. Not only can this become a considerable burden for you, it can backfire as family members may begin to take your peacekeeping efforts for granted. Knowing that you'll intervene, they may be less careful to keep their aggressions in check. You unwittingly contribute to the fusion in your family as a result, and you feel even more burdened and resentful as you dig yourself even deeper into your peacekeeping role.

The Tower of Strength Role: You're looked at as the stable one, the one to consult in times of need, and while this can be good for your self-esteem on one level, it can cause you considerable anxiety on another—especially if you have doubts that you're deserving of the role. You may find yourself caught between feeling disrespect for the weak ones around you and disrespect for *yourself* for feeling like an impostor. Your real identity gets usurped either way, as you are not free to decide for yourself just how "strong" you really want to be.

The Weakling Role: You grew up feeling like the runt of the litter as a child, and the feeling is still with you as an adult. You feel in constant need of approval, encouragement, and support, and you feel especially weak because you're not getting this support from your depressed partner. You're in competition with your loved one for who's in greater need of being coddled, and it's adding to the fusion in your relationship, which is weakening both of you even more.

The Worrier Role: Someone has to do the worrying, you feel, and since it can't be your partner—*who's your main source of worry*—it has to be you. Again, this is apt to be a repeat performance of anxieties you may have felt as a child. If your family had financial difficulties or your parents were abusive to you or to each other, you're going to be especially anxious about these difficulties disturbing you all over again as an adult. But worry sometimes creates its own fears. Chronic worrying can fuel the very fusion that it dreads.

The "Wise Ass" Role: This role may appear to be an offensive one, but it usually originates as a defensive one. If one or both of your parents was especially punitive, you may have learned to protect yourself by "back talking," regardless of the further trouble it would bring for you. It was your way of keeping your dignity if not the household peace. So what happens if you wind up having to cope with a loved one who's as abusive as your parents were? You come out swinging like you always have. And fusion, of course, becomes the main event.

The Role of the "Bitch" or "Nag": You strongly disapprove of your depressed loved one's behavior and you let it be known. As with the other roles we've discussed, this could be a repetition of a role you felt you had to play in response to an especially unruly family member as a child, and the role is being resurrected in your present relationship with your depressed partner. All I can say is, be mindful of the influence. You're going to have to learn to discard the "bitch" role in order to defuse in the manner we discussed in Chapter 4. "Bitch" might best be thought of as "botch" when it comes to the successful deployment of defusion strategies.

ROLE-PLAYING IN ACTION: THE CASE OF HERB AND PEARL

If you find it a bit farfetched that fusion should be able to force people to resume roles learned during childhood, I can assure you it is not. People rarely realize they're regressing into these roles, but that only makes their regression more insidious. You can be totally immersed in a past role without a clue that it's happening, and continue to believe that you're reacting rationally and justifiably to your current situation. The case of Herb and Pearl illustrates this danger.

Herb and Pearl have been married for thirty-five years, the first two of which had been storybook. Herb showered Pearl with everything she wanted—affection, support, praise, and great sex. She knew he had flaws, but she was willing to overlook them because she was so elated to escape the highly toxic relationship she had been experiencing since adolescence with her stepmother.

Pearl's stepmother had been harsh and at times even cruel, and though Pearl's father was kind and loving, his career in sales had kept him largely absent. Pearl and her stepmother, as a result, had been alone to fuse tooth and nail for nearly twenty years, and the fusion took its toll. Pearl had precious little self-esteem, which is why she fell so unconditionally for Herb. Sure, he drank too much and tended to be a braggart, but at least he treated her with respect. Or at least in the beginning he did.

As their marriage wore on, Herb wore down. He had set extremely high standards for himself in business, and when the economic instability of the late 70s and early 80s turned his world upside down professionally, it also capsized him emotionally. His drinking escalated, and he became abusive and sometimes even violent. It was happening to Pearl all over again!

Pearl had moved from the frying pan into the proverbial fire. She was again in a fused relationship with a monster, but rather than reacting rationally and trying to remedy her situation, she regressed to her childhood role as the defenseless "victim" and took everything Herb could dish out.

And why not? It was the only response she knew. She found herself being pulled right back into the role of the victimized little girl. It didn't even occur to her that Herb could be suffering from a depression. His behavior was similar to what she had grown up with, so why should she see it as a medical condition capable of being cured?

Pearl's story illustrates all too well the learned-role phenomenon. Her fused relationship with Herb had reduced her to her most familiar—and least rational—level of emotional functioning. In the heat of battle, she would retreat to the only role—that of the "victim"—that she knew.

This is why the defusion strategies we discussed in Chapters 4 and 5 are so critical. By bringing an end to fusion, they help bring an end to destructive role-playing. They break you away from your old, reactionary ways of behaving so that you can be free to develop new, more *rational* ways directed by a calm intellect, ways that will more accurately reflect the person *you* really want to be rather than the person fusion has been *forcing* you to be. Trust me when I say that there is no way you will be able to spiral up to the higher emotional ground I'm talking about in this chapter if you stay fused. You will not be able to generate the self-confidence, the self-esteem, the energy, or the insight as long as fusion is keeping you a prisoner of your past ways.

BECOMING BETTER "COORDINATED"

"But doctor, what if the role you say I'm playing is the only role I know? Can I really expect to become a different person, especially after being this way my whole life?"

That was Pearl's question to me after she had made some progress in defusing, and it was a good one. What potential is there for change when you've been a certain way your whole life? Can you really expect to discard old roles and develop a new and improved self-image?

"You can if you dedicate yourself," I told Pearl. The key to your ability to change is your willingness to change, to do whatever it takes to achieve a healthier self. And to do that you must be ready to tolerate the guilt and the fear that stand in your way. If you have been able to separate from your primary family in a physical sense, you have the ability to separate from the roles you played within that family in an emotional sense. The problem is that many of us simply never try. We leave the nest, but we don't leave the roles we played within that nest. We go from being children to being adults without ever really re-equipping ourselves with the emotional tools we need to deal effectively with our adult relationships. Think of some of the phrases that we commonly use when we find ourselves immersed in fusion skirmishes:

"You're acting like a baby."

"You can be so immature."

"When are you ever going to grow up?"

These phrases pinpoint the lack of emotional development that so often is at the heart of our adult conflicts. We really *haven't* grown up. We simply revert back into the behavior patterns that we learned first and know best, especially when our "emotional intelligence" is being reduced to its lowest levels by fusion.

When I delivered this speech to Pearl, she seemed a bit shocked. At 55, she didn't expect to be told it was time for her to start acting her age. Yet fundamentally, that's what her failure had been. She had never displayed the imagination, or put forth the effort, or taken the risks needed to develop her self-image beyond what had been forged by her upbringing. She had simply carried on, allowing herself to revert back to her old childhood role as the "victim," regardless of what new crisis would arise.

Might you be guilty of a similar kind of emotional backtracking?

Very possibly, and especially if fusion has been predominant in your life. If you were forced to witness or participate in fusion as a child, and you have gone on to become involved in a fused relationship as an adult, your self-esteem and emotional growth have been under the influence of a powerfully stifling force for most of your life. Fusion drives you into a mode of sheer emotional survival, remember, where you shut down your rational intellect and your more primitive gut reactions become your primary coping strategies. Self-exploration and hence self-discovery can be hard to come by in such a combative environment.

INDIVIDUATION = IMAGINATION + DETERMINATION

There's good news in this bad news, however, because fusion—as we've seen—can be escaped. And when it is, opportunities open up for self-discovery that for so long had been suppressed. Some of the emotional awakenings I have seen in people once free of the tyranny of fusion have been truly remarkable.

When I told this to Pearl, she finally seemed encouraged. But I had to caution her, as I caution you, that the kind of emotional awakenings I'm talking about do not come with the push of a button. They take work. And they take vision. And they take being realistic. This last component—what I call the "acceptance" factor—may be the most important of all, because acceptance is really the end goal of the spiraling-up process. Yes, you must work to visualize a healthy self and then move toward making that vision a reality, but you also must learn to accept what cannot be changed. Your own assets and limitations as well as the strengths and weaknesses of those closest to you must be incorporated into your expectations of life and love. Only by accepting what *can't* be changed can you arrive at inner peace.

But enough theory. Let's get down to the specifics of how such a journey toward greater inner peace might be approached.

I used to have a golf coach in college who would say that "what the mind can conceive, the body can achieve," and while I was never able to convince my putter of that, he had a good point. Before you can embark on a program of change, you've got to have a clear mental picture of what those changes are going to be. First see yourself in the past, and decide where your problem areas have been. What self-doubts have you had? What fears? What sources of guilt?

From the past, move to the present. What currently do you see as your weak points, and to what degree might you realistically expect they can be improved?

And finally, the future—both the near future and the distant future. What sort of progress are you going to expect from yourself? How will your life be different six weeks from now? Six months from now? Six years from now? The more clearly you can envision the steps that are going to take you where you want to go, the better your chances are going to be of getting there.

Balancing Your Three Spheres

I'm also going to suggest that you begin thinking of yourself in each of three different life spheres—your work, your relationships, and your physical health. This can help you with your self-improvement efforts in an organizational sense, but it also can show you where you may be out of balance. You may feel confident and very much on track in your professional life, but have difficulty in dealing with your emotions, and/or harbor feelings of guilt for being negligent of your body. Or you may be an outright fitness buff with a reasonably good level of emotional adjustment who's being nagged by feelings of deficiency at work. I have found that very few people feel equally at peace in each of their professional, emotional, and health/fitness spheres. They may feel highly confident and self-directed in one or even two, but feel very deficient in the other. The result is much like a tire that can't roll smoothly because of a lump. No matter how flawless the rest of the tire, it will produce a bumpy ride as long as the lump is there.

You've got to be well-rounded, in short, if you want your life to go smoothly. You've got to have an integrated vision of yourself that is consistent in each of your three spheres if you're going to achieve the overriding self-confidence and inner peace that are the goals of the spiraling-up process. Here are some questions you should ask yourself as a way of determining just how balanced—or imbalanced—your three spheres are. The more "yes" answers you can give, the better.

Your Professional Sphere

▲ Is the image you're projecting to your associates at work consistent with the kind of person you feel you really are?

▲ Is your job satisfying and meaningful to you?

▲ Do you feel you're good at what you do?

▲ Is your job helping your self-esteem?

▲ Do you feel you have enough room for advancement in your job to suit your goals?

▲ Do you feel you're making enough money to suit your vision of your life-style?

Your Emotional Sphere

▲ Do you feel good about your role as a spouse?

▲ Do you feel you have assets to bring to the people closest to you?

▲ Are you willing to accept that you may have limitations in dealing emotionally with those closest to you, and are you willing to work on them?

▲ Do you feel your family members are perceiving you as you want to be perceived?

▲ Are your "nonnegotiable" emotional needs being met in your close relationships (see Chapter 7)?

Your Health/Fitness Sphere

▲ Do you feel you're doing enough to safeguard your health?

▲ Do you feel you're in the physical condition you would like to be?

▲ Are you at peace with your appearance and body image?

▲ Do you feel your physical appearance reflects the kind of person you are?

▲ Do you feel you're doing all you can to be attractive sexually?

As you can see, "yes" answers will indicate that your images of yourself in your three spheres are reasonably consistent, and that's good. It means your energies are being spent in an integrated rather than fragmented fashion and that you're being motivated by your own realistic visions of yourself rather than by the expectations of others. "No" answers, however, indicate that just the opposite is true—that your sense of identity is being divided and that your motivations are not your own. Your self-esteem and your potential for happiness are being limited as a result.

BECOMING BETTER COORDINATED: THE CASE OF ALEX

To illustrate the importance of achieving a good coordination between your professional, emotional, and physical spheres, I'd like to present the case of Alex. Alex was quite "uncoordinated" when he first came to me, but we were able to get him to spiral up to a much higher level of coordination by using my three-spheres approach.

Alex was highly confident and dynamic in his professional life as a vice president of a major advertising firm, but his emotional life was a shambles. He told me in our first session that he felt like "a pathetic failure" both as a husband and a father as his marriage of twenty-five years to his chronically depressed wife had been a veritable fusion fandango. His wife was rarely happy with anything or anyone. If she wasn't finding fault with Alex or the children, she was finding fault with herself. Alex would respond to his wife's negativity in the only way he knew how—by trying to console her. He found himself playing the role of nursemaid to his wife, a repeat performance, I soon learned, of a similar role he had played with his alcoholic mother when he was a child. His wife invariably would be insulted by his condescending efforts, however, and the fusion between them would only burn brighter.

"What in God's name am I supposed to do?" he asked me during our first meeting. "Everything I try just seems to make our situation worse."

Alex had developed a hefty drinking problem in response to his marital frustrations, and he was smoking upwards of two packs of cigarettes a day. He clearly was a man out of sync, a man trying to medicate his psychic pain as his vision of himself as a highly successful business person clashed thunderously with his woeful lack of success as a husband. His attempts to deal with his pain were only fragmenting him further, moreover, as his abuse of his health was a blatant contradiction to the image of durability and power he projected at work. The conflict between his three spheres was creating a kind of friction that quite literally was beginning to wear him out.

"So do I get some sort of mental lube job?" Alex asked jokingly when I explained to him his conflicts.

"You might think of it that way," I answered. "We're going to have to eliminate the incongruence between the three major aspects of your life. We've got to get them all working toward the same goals."

Step one, I decided was to get Alex to defuse from the toxic relationship he was having with his wife. He had to take responsibility for his own actions and stop passing them off as justifiable reactions to his wife's illness. This would mean acknowledging that his drinking and smoking were addictive behaviors that were imprisoning him in his dilemma far more than providing an escape, and that he would have to be willing to face the real reasons he was allowing himself to stay in such a mutually harmful relationship.

As we explored Alex's past, it became more clear that his role of playing nursemaid to his alcoholic mother had been coming back to haunt him more than he knew. Fusion was causing him to revert back to the behavior he knew best, that of the selfless martyr willing to risk his own emotional health in trying to help someone he perceived to be in great need.

And yet Alex's "help" was producing all the wrong effects, just as it had with his mother. It was allowing his wife to stay sick, just as it had allowed his mother to stay sick. Alex needed to face this. And he needed to face why he was feeling compelled to play nursemaid to his wife in the first place. He was acting out of insecurity. His fused relationship with his mother had left him with very little self-esteem. Despite feeling highly confident in his business dealings, he felt confused and afraid when it came to dealing with personal relationships. In truth, he was afraid of losing his wife, which is why he was unable to deal with her in a strong and decisive manner. But as I told him, he would have to risk that loss if he was ever going to have a chance of finding himself.

There would be no way Alex could adequately coordinate the three spheres of his life as long as he continued the role of the weak, coddling, alcoholic husband. We first tried a period of defusion where Alex disengaged from his wife's depressed moods, and while this helped Alex begin to see himself more clearly, it did not have an equally beneficial effect on his wife. She continued in her negative and faultfinding ways, so I suggested Alex discuss a therapeutic separation with his wife. He resisted at first, but I told him he was going to have to remove himself from his wife's disruptive influence if he was going to be able to unify his three spheres. There was no way the man at home could become the man at work as long as home was so toxic.

So they separated. At my suggestion, his wife continued treatment with her therapist, and Alex continued his sessions with me. Within several months, not surprisingly, Alex's wife began to improve as much as Alex. Alex's contribution to the fusion in their relationship had been blocking her from being a healthier person, as much as her depression had been blocking him. Only in his absence could she begin to see herself as functional, and begin doing what had to be done to make her healthier self-visions a reality. One year after their separation, Alex and his wife reunited, each far more "whole" for having broken apart. Their separation had allowed them to develop in each of their three spheres so that in being better balanced as individuals, they could be better balanced as a couple.

FOLLOW YOUR VISIONS, NOT YOUR INSTINCTS

What Alex did was not easy. But, then, taking yourself apart so that you can put yourself back together never is. What kept

Alex on track was his determination to follow a clear vision he kept in mind of what he wanted for himself and for his marriage. Yes, he would have to be realistic about what he could expect from his wife, but he also had to remain true to his "nonnegotiable" needs. He needed a companion who could participate in his success, who could socialize with him, and who could have enough confidence in herself to be supportive of his strengths rather than feel threatened by them. Many times while defusing, and even after they had reunited following their separation, Alex had been tempted to fall back into his old role as the selfless caretaker, but he fought these urges. He felt guilt and even fear that he might not be doing the right thing. But he stuck to his mental visions of what he wanted his life to be in each of his three spheres. He kept calm and succeeded in acting in a well-adjusted manner, even if he didn't always *feel* well adjusted. And his determination paid off!

Being happy and well-adjusted in each of the three spheres of our lives is not easy. If it were, we wouldn't have the epidemic of mood disturbances and addictive disorders that we do. And yet you can be happy and well adjusted if you are willing to understand and then fight the forces that discourage you—that's what you must always keep in mind. Very few people achieve inner peace without concentrated effort. That might seem contradictory, but it's not. Happiness, stability, and emotional adjustment, like anything else that is precious, take effort that must be sustained over time.

RATIONAL, NOT REACTIONARY

But why should happiness be so difficult? Why can't it just come naturally?

Because reacting naturally, unfortunately, usually is precisely what *prevents* us from being happy. When we react naturally, from our "gut," we revert back to behaviors we learned in the past, as I've said, and these behaviors often are inappropriate and unhelpful for the situations that provoke us. Dysfunc-tional family upbringings, re-created through fused, destruc-tive relationships with our depressed loved ones, frequently cause our natural reactions to highly charged emotional situa-tions to be faulty and destructive, as we attempt to perpetuate former behavior patterns rather than working to create new ones more suitable for dealing with the situations we face. If we can accept this tendency in ourselves and learn to guard against it, we bring good relationships—and good emotional stability—that much closer.

Is this to say we need to become emotional robots, automa-tons capable of controlling our emotions like the channels on our TVs?

In a sense, yes. Emotions out of control would not be a problem if they were truly honest emotions, but usually they are not. They're "impostor" emotions reflecting past influences, which may have very little to do with the current circumstances that incite them. This means that by giving into such impostor emotions, you're actually moving away from where you need to go to communicate effectively. You may think you're speaking from your heart when you blow your stack, but you're actually speaking from the fears, wounds, and distortions of your dis-tant past. You're responding to a myriad of emotions from your early life experiences that are merging with your reactions to the reality of the present.

You must not let them. You must come to understand the forces that compel you to behave in the maladaptive, spon-taneous ways that you do, and then learn to control your reactions to these spontaneous feelings. If your reaction to being provoked is to withdraw and feel paralyzed by indecision or fear, this is merely another form of a maladaptive response, a gut reaction likely to have its roots in the learned behaviors of your childhood. You must learn to manage and modify this kind of "destructive spontaneity," just as much as the type that slams doors and breaks dishes. Gut reactions, whether ag-gressive or passive, rarely make for open and honest communication. Just because you feel something doesn't make it legitimate or worthy of being expressed.

I often tell my patients an experience I had with my father as a teenager that makes just this point. I was asking Dad for a loan to buy a car, a loan that I would pay back—with interest—by using the car to drive to a job after school. Seemingly without thinking, he said no, and it upset me because he could give me no good reason for his answer. We argued for several minutes as I gave him all the details of how the payback schedule would work—and to my surprise, he suddenly agreed.

"I'm sorry I reacted that way, but you should know for the future that my gut reactions to issues about money are often wrong," he said.

I gained a lot of respect for my father when he spoke those words. Not only did he show that he was willing really to listen to what I had been saying, but he was willing to admit he had been wrong, that he had allowed his gut instincts to overrule his more rational intellect. This is precisely the kind of admission that people who spiral up become capable of making. They begin to understand and identify their gut reactions enough to supersede them. They allow reason rather than just raw emotion to rule.

THE RESISTANCE TO EXPECT

When I told Pearl the story about my father, she made a good point. She said it was easy for my dad to do what he had done because he was up against no resistance from me. I, after all, wanted nothing more than for him to be objective.

Pearl's husband Herb, by contrast, would fight her tooth and nail when she would try to show the objectivity my father had shown. "It's almost as though he gets scared when I start acting too sensibly," she said. "That's when he gets even more wild and irrational. I think he feels more comfortable when I'm confused and upset."

"And why shouldn't he?" I responded. "Your confusion

allows him to avoid facing his own confusion—confusion about how he really feels and what he really wants. He feels least vulnerable when things are going badly between the two of you because it keeps each of you in the roles he's been used to."

I went on to explain to Pearl that the resistance she was getting from Herb was very common. Any movement toward greater emotional stability on the part of one member of a fused couple gets perceived as a threat by the other because it violates the accepted "order." You must be prepared to meet and overcome this resistance from your loved one if you're going to succeed in your spiraling-up efforts. You must remain true to pursuing *your* vision of the person *you* want to be, regardless of how you may feel swayed by the criticisms, guilt trips, and expectations or needs of others. Initially, much like defusing, this may require sacrificing some of the closeness you wish you could have with the people around you, but it's a sacrifice you must be willing to make if you're going to gain the autonomy that spiraling up requires.

Pearl took my advice and things eventually worked out very well for her. She created an emotional distance from Herb that allowed her to focus on herself as it also forced Herb to focus on himself. Pearl felt guilty, afraid, and lonely at times, but she stayed motivated by keeping a clear mental picture of the strong and independent person she wanted to be. She aligned her "determination with her imagination," as we decided, and it produced results. She got a job as an assistant at a day-care center, she joined a weight-loss program, and she began taking a photography course at night. Herb ridiculed her for her self-improvement efforts at first, but she hung tough. She was determined to spiral up, whether Herb would be able to join her or not.

Spiraling Up Together: Doubling the Fun

"But I'm not sure I want to grow away from my husband even if it is in my best interest. We have so many years together, and there are the children to think about. It's just not easy to risk leaving so much behind, no matter what the benefits might be for me personally."

Many of my patients express that concern, and it's certainly a legitimate one. Achieving emotional growth can be hard enough without having to worry that it's going to separate you from the things you value most.

To which I respond: Sometimes you have to risk losing in order to gain. If there is anything worth saving in your relationship with your loved one, it will survive and even benefit from your spiraling-up journey. The only requirement will be that you look back over your shoulder occasionally to make sure your partner isn't falling too far behind. This will assume, of course, that your loved one has agreed to undergo treatment for his or her depression, or that he or she is making significant progress on his own. There is no way you can spiral up as a couple until both of you have defused and until your loved one's mood disturbance has at least started to lift.

Once these conditions have been met, however, a much improved relationship can lie ahead. Yes, you will have created an emotional distance between you and your loved one by defusing, but once the defusion process has been complete, and you are no longer reacting spontaneously and irrationally to one another, you will be ready to narrow the distance you've created and move closer together. You should go slowly and carefully, because the wounds you have suffered may still be sensitive, but your reunion can be a very successful one if approached in the right way. You will have learned a great deal about yourselves by defusing, and this knowledge can lay the foundation for a relationship far superior to what you had before fusion began.

Certain ground rules for this new relationship must be followed, however, because fusion is not like a physical disease in that once cured, it is cured for good. It can return at any time if either of you lets down your guard, so please keep that in mind as you begin your reunion process. If you can abide by the following ground rules, I can guarantee that your relationship will be greatly improved despite the hardship it has endured.

▲ *Accept each other for who you are, but also work toward who you want to be.* This means being realistic about each other's weaknesses as well as being optimistic about your strengths. Fusion has shown each of you your absolute worst traits, but in so doing it has revealed where each of you needs work. Use this information to build a better relationship in a mutually supportive way. Insist that each of you strive to reach your maximum level of emotional adjustment while at the same time showing understanding, compassion, and empathy for limitations stemming from old emotional wounds.

▲ *Consider yourself equals.* Feelings of inequality may have fueled the fusion between you in the first place, so it's important to be on an equal footing as you start out anew. There may be lingering feelings of guilt or blame for what you've been through, but they have no place in your relationship.

▲ *Look to the future, not the past.* You will only risk rekindling fusion by reanalyzing the past, so set your sights forward. Form visions of the opportunities that lie ahead for you now that you're finally working as a team. Compliment yourselves on your progress, and don't berate yourselves for temporary regressions.

▲ *Use humor to smooth over the rough spots.* This isn't to say you should joke your way around major roadblocks, but it does mean learning to laugh at minor snags. You generate a positive spirit when you can laugh at each other's flaws—particularly your own.

▲ *Don't be afraid to make rules.* There can be no future for your relationship if it's not satisfying your most essential "nonnegotiable" emotional needs (discussed in Chapter 7), so don't be afraid to establish whatever rules may be necessary for guaranteeing these needs get met.

▲ *Don't be afraid to share.* Maybe a reluctance in this area sparked the fusion in your relationship from the start. If you and your loved one are going to spiral up together, you're going to have to learn the value of sharing your present joys as well as your future visions. Just as negative feelings can be contagious, so can positive feelings, but they can't spread unless they're expressed.

▲ *Respect your needs for individual time.* A relationship doesn't have to be a close one in time and space to be a close one emotionally. Many couples spiral up together in a spiritual sense precisely *because* they've learned to give each other the independence they need. They're there for each other in the ways and at the times they need to be. Don't feel your relationship is necessarily deficient if it seems to need this kind of space. Remember, the emotional distance that extinguishes fusion is the *right* emotional distance for you, even if it creates a relationship that doesn't resemble the relationships of friends, relatives, or leading characters in the world of entertainment.

▲ *Keep on guard.* Fusion, remember, is not like a physical ailment whose cure can be final. Regardless of how well each of you has mastered the defusion process and have begun your spiraling-up journey, there will be times when you're tempted to react in ways capable of rekindling fusion flare-ups. If it happens, don't panic. Just have the confidence that *whichever* one of you is in the better mood and coping more effectively at the moment will assume the lead in keeping skirmishes to a minimum. It may be you one time and your partner the next, but what's important is that you stay committed *as a team* to preventing fusion's return.

▲ *Avoid old roles.* This may be your most effective strategy for staying free of fusion. You must not slip back into the old role or roles that fusion forced you to play. You must stay focused on the visions you have of the "new" you, someone self-confident and self-directed enough to respond rationally rather than emotionally to whatever crisis may arise. Not only will this help you with your own metamorphosis, it will help your partner with his. If you can stay committed to being the "new" you, your partner will find it easier to be the "new" him, and your new roles will go on to become mutually reinforcing. This is the basic chemistry of the spiraling-up process. Just as fusion causes emotional chain reactions that destroy self-esteem, spiraling up causes chain reactions that build self-esteem. Once in its grasp, you and your loved one will find each other bringing out your best rather than worst traits.

Bringing Back the Intimacy

"But will spiraling up bring out greater intimacy, Dr. Podell? I see how it can build greater emotional independence and self-esteem, but are these really the ways to bring back the closeness my husband and I once had or would like to have?"

I get asked that question frequently, and I answer it in this say: True intimacy *cannot exist* without self-esteem. Not until you feel secure about yourself can you feel you have anything to give, and not until you give can you expect to get. Intimacy requires more strength than many people realize—and it's precisely this strength that spiraling up from the ashes of fusion can produce.

By learning to defuse, you learn to define more clearly who you really are, and your loved one learns to do the same. This allows each of you to develop the self-confidence to take the kind of emotional risks that true intimacy requires. You learn to reach out for things you might not have had the courage to reach out for before, and you learn to offer things you might not have thought you could offer before. Your relationship—as a system—becomes more confident of itself, and this allows you to do the kind of emotional exploration that true intimacy is really all about.

But more than just self-confidence bring couples closer when they spiral up—feelings of *safety* and *trust* also come into play. Having survived fusion, couples who spiral up have the advantage of knowing so much more about each other than before fusion began. All the ghosts and dirty laundry have been revealed, so there's no more fear or mistrust based on the unknown. Couples learn to accept each other based on the whole truth and nothing but the truth, and this creates new standards and new possibilities for their relationships.

It might even be considered a hidden blessing of fusion that it reveals so much truth about its victims. Knowing the truth about each other, establishing the right emotional distance by setting limits, and knowing that the *two* of you can handle a tough situation without exploding into a fusion eruption or separating in cold silence builds emotional safety. It is from this feeling of greater safety that trust is born, the trust you need to achieve intimacy in its highest form.

Spiraling Up in Action: Karen and Paul Revisited

To make sure that spiraling up comes across to you as more than just a philosophical concept, I'd like to conclude this chapter with an account of the process in action. Most of the couples I treat go on to spiral up to a significant degree, but I've chosen the case of Karen and Paul, whom you first met in Chapter 3, because their growth was especially dramatic.

To refresh your memory, Paul was the talented, but struggling, screenwriter who was abusing alcohol, marijuana, and even exercise to help him deny his depression. His wife, Karen, was having emotional problems of her own, and found herself hopelessly dependent on Paul, despite seeing him as irresponsible and emotionally disturbed. This caused her great anxiety, which she expressed by constantly berating Paul to change his aberrant ways.

My first job was to get Karen to defuse. She needed to see that her attempts to control Paul were actually attempts to control her own life, which she felt was threatened by her inability to support herself financially, her fear of being abandoned, and her dwindling confidence in her attractiveness to the opposite sex.

This was not an easy job, as Karen spent our first sessions focusing on how immature, irresponsible, and "sick" Paul was. She felt his problems were to blame for her problems: a classic fusion scenario, which I had to convince her was very counterproductive. We needed to focus on *her:* on why she felt afraid of being abandoned, and why she felt inadequate and guilty.

Once we were able to separate these issues from her concerns about Paul, Karen began to feel less overwhelmed. We started mapping out specific strategies for how she could change the things about her life that worried her. She needed more meaningful friendships so that she wouldn't feel so dependent emotionally on Paul, and she needed a more secure career than her real estate job so that she wouldn't feel so dependent on him financially. At the same time, she needed to realize that her attempts to control Paul were only making him step farther out of line. He was like the proverbial bar of wet soap, I told her—more apt to escape her grasp with every tightening of her grip.

Paul's reaction to Karen's new hands-off approach didn't surprise me. He totally ignored it at first, thinking she was just going through a passing phase. But when he realized her newfound independence was for real, he rebelled by indulging in his addictions even more. He attempted to regain her attention by winning back her wrath—but it didn't fly.

Karen entered his office one evening and announced calmly and caringly that she still loved him and probably always would, that she found him physically attractive and emotionally sensitive, and that she had great respect and even envy for his brilliance as a writer. However, she was convinced that he was suffering from a serious emotional disorder that was causing him to waste himself; that he had both depression and substance-abuse problems that were tragically limiting him as a writer, a husband, and a father. She told him she would have to distance herself from him in every way possible if he could not gather the courage to face his problems by seeking professional help. "I love you too much to continue to watch you destroy yourself, and I care too much for *myself* to go down with you," were her finishing words as she gently pulled his office door shut.

The impact of Karen's words initially did more damage than good. Paul spent that night at a friend's house, where he indulged in every intoxicant the two of them could muster. But as he awoke the next morning in a strange bed, in a strange house, and feeling like death warmed over, a sense of isolation came over him that finally was just too much to bear. He called me shortly before noon that day, and we scheduled an appointment for the following week.

Karen's defusion had worked for both of them. By focusing on building her own self-confidence and managing her own problems instead of Paul's, she not only helped herself, but conquered Paul's resistance and denial with her honesty and compassion. She no longer gave him reason to consider her his enemy, so with no more enemy, he had no more reason to fight. His only adversary now was himself.

Therapy progressed slowly at first with Paul. He had a lot of pride and denial, which were evident in his skepticism about the seriousness of his depression and also the severity of the addictions he was using to mask his depression. He preferred to think of himself as the soul-searching artist who used alcohol and marijuana merely to get in closer touch with his feelings. He couldn't believe me when I told him that his use of alcohol and pot were actually helping him avoid his true feelings; that they were numbing him to his present depression as well as to experiences from his past that probably were contributing to his depression. Toward the end of our third session together, I suggested we walk into my waiting room, where I have a large mirror. I asked him to take a look and tell me what he saw.

He said he saw someone who was trying as hard as he could to be the best writer he could be. I said I saw a man who was trying as hard as he could to avoid being the best writer he could be, a man who was putting himself at every possible disadvantage. I told him he was impairing his ability to concentrate not just by muddying his mind with alcohol and pot, but by insisting on maintaining a highly turbulent relationship with his potentially very supportive wife. And why?

Because he was using these disadvantages as his excuse for not achieving greater success. "Failure doesn't hurt so much when you can tell yourself you're not functioning at your full potential," I told him. And for the first time, I could see in his eyes that I was getting through.

Therapy started going much better after that talk in front of the mirror. I convinced Paul to begin attending AA meetings to help control his substance abuse, and after a few weeks of sobriety he agreed to begin a course of medication therapy for his depression. Three weeks after starting he antidepressant medication, he reported a mental clarity and intellectual energy that he said he hadn't experienced since his days as an honor student in high school. We began exploring his childhood in great and highly illuminating depth and were able to link it not just to his depression, but to his addictive behavior and his fears of failing in his career. Paul had been one of seven children raised by two alcoholic parents who would praise their children when sober, but cut them to the bone when drunk. Paul was left with precious little sense of identity, self-esteem, and trust in other people as a result.One brother and a sister also had suffered from fairly serious depressions, so clearly there was depression in his genetic heritage. Paul found it fascinating how we were finally getting all the pieces of his confusing puzzle to fit.

I felt confident about inviting Karen into our sessions at this point, because Paul told me that their fusion had pretty much ended. Both were focusing on their own needs and goals, and there was relative peace for the first time in over three years. But would this peaceful coexistence be enough? They were friends, and even occasionally sex partners, but not really lovers. Both were beginning to wonder if such a compromised relationship would be enough.

Karen, especially, felt it was time to strive for more. "We're getting along," she said during our first joint session, "but we're living essentially separate lives. I was hoping our marriage could be more."

Paul agreed. "It's as though we're both holding back out of fear. Isn't there a way to move beyond this?"

I immediately told them how encouraged I was by their remarks. They missed their old romantic intimacy. The long defusing process had restored the peace, but peace was not turning out to be enough. They had higher expectations of marriage. They wanted back the spontaneity and passion they had known in their 20s. Could such a relationship really be possible, after all they had been through?

I told them it could. But there would be limits, and there would be risks. By letting down their defusion guards, they'd be rendering themselves vulnerable to many of the same demons that had haunted their relationship in the past. They could never forget what each of them had done to stop the fusion. Had each of them learned enough about themselves and about each other to build a new relationship that could survive these dangers, a relationship that could be realistic about the amount of growth each of them could expect to achieve, a relationship built upon acceptance as much as change? That really would be the key issue. Were they ready to accept each other despite the limitations that their years of fusion had made all too apparent, and define a common vision? Yes, each of them was working to correct their past faults, but such makeovers are never complete. There would have to be considerable elements of both tolerance and trust if their relationship was going to regain the confidence true intimacy requires. There could be no more second-guessing about motives, degree of commitment, or who might be trying to gain the upper hand. They were going to have to enter into the "new" relationship as total equals, each equally to credit and/or to blame for whatever success or failures they might encounter.

When I delivered this message, I could see that my words were merely words to them—philosophical and psychological concepts. As is often the case, it took a crisis to truly test their ability to spiral up to higher levels of intimacy and emotional health.

Paul had been working hard on a script for a TV series. The stakes were high because if the producer liked his work, it might mean a chance to become a staff writer. This could have been the best chance he'd had in years to elevate his career status, not to mention provide the financial security that the family needed.

Paul was in agony over the project—scared of failing, maybe secretly scared of succeeding, but he kept it all bottled inside him and didn't reach out for any support. Under the pressure, he regressed to his former dysfunctional role, which left him without any of the healthy coping strategies he had developed since starting therapy and joining AA. And that's when Karen found the bag of marijuana in the bathroom cabinet. He'd been smoking again. She had suspected it. He was sleeping late and seemed much more moody and withdrawn, but now she had the proof.

Her gut reaction was predictable. She flipped out. She brought the bag into the living room where he was watching television and started screaming, "What the hell is this? You're a goddamn junkie. You can't do this teleplay, can you? You're smoking because you're running away, you're scared, and you just don't have the guts to face it. You don't care about me or the kids, you just escape into that sick drug world and hide."

Paul was knocked for a loop. He simply got up, walked into his office, and slammed the door. He was wounded, hurt, and of course, deep down, he didn't want to deal with the reality of what she was saying. He thought about leaving, about getting away and staying with some friends until he could get enough money together to move out.

Meanwhile, Paul's exit to the den had given Karen a chance

to calm down and let her intellect start to function again. She had been cold, cruel, and insensitive. She had also been scared to death by Paul's relapse. She went into the den and sat down. She saw a glass of vodka and found Paul weeping.

"I'm sorry, Paul. It was wrong of me to react that way. Obviously, you're scared about this script. I'm scared about it, too. Not that I'm scared you can't write it, because you're the best damn writer around. But I've been scared because I'm not sure if you can handle the pressure and that you might start drinking again, and we'd be back where we were. And that means I don't get to be taken care of and we don't get the big house in Beverly Hills and all that kind of crap—all the crap that belongs to me and my hang-ups and has nothing to do with you. But you didn't reach out for help and deal with your problems in a healthy way, and when I see the drugs and alcohol I get frightened."

"Thanks Karen. Jesus, you're a great lady. What you said was right. I am scared, and I wasn't coping well, and instead of getting help, I started to regress and use the pot to help me get some courage and some creativity. And that's not only dangerous for me but totally insensitive to you and the kids."

After acknowledging their mutual participation in this recurrent fusion eruption, they had probably the most important conversation of their lives.

"I've been thinking, Karen, maybe this screenwriting isn't for me. I know I'm a good writer, but I'm starting to realize that it takes more than good writing to make it in Hollywood. It takes a certain emotional makeup that I don't have, and in many ways, I don't even want. And putting myself under this pressure and feeling like a failure is crazy. I'm tired of trying to prove myself. The important things in my life are being healthy and having a good relationship with you and the children, and we can't have a solid family if I'm crazed or drugged because of work."

Karen quickly responded, "Now come on, don't give up on yourself, you're as talented as anyone."

Paul looked at Karen with a hurt, angry stare, and she could see that her comments had injured him rather than encouraged him. And she knew why. "I'm sorry, Paul, I agree with what you're saying. We've both had dreams that didn't come true, but the most important thing in my life is having a healthy relationship with you and the children. Whatever you decide to do, I'm ready to go with you and support you."

And that was the day they spiraled up. Each of them individuated enough to accept responsibility for their own problems, their own fears, their own limitations, and each other's limitations. And they now had agreed that they shared a common vision and were ready to move on to a different life together—a life of partnership and sound mental health, a life where they knew their basic values, had their own visions of life, and strove for what they each could achieve.

That was three years ago. I got a note from Karen last Christmas. The whole family relocated to the East Coast shortly after their breakthrough conversation. Paul was working as a creative writer in an advertising firm. He had recently been promoted to vice president and was earning an excellent salary, and Karen had started her own consulting business, which was doing quite well. They were enjoying a warm, close relationship and the children were happy and doing well in school. Paul had had over three years of sobriety and had not had any recurrences of his depression.

In Conclusion

Can you expect to spiral up to the heights achieved by Karen and Paul? I'm going to be the realist again. You can if you're willing to work for it. There is no way you can spiral up to the higher emotional ground I'm talking about unless you defuse. If you still have doubts about what defusion involves, please refer back to Chapters 4, 5, and 6. Defusion is so vital because it requires you to exercise the very fundamentals of which happiness is made. It requires you to work toward greater self-understanding, greater independence, greater self-acceptance, and greater self-esteem. It also requires you to have a clear and realistic vision of what you want from life, and a clear and realistic plan for how you're going to get it. That's about as succinct a prescription for happiness as I can write.

But I'm sure you still have some questions, so let's conclude by stepping into my office. The issues I'll be addressing in this final chapter are those most often raised by patients as they begin implementing my program.

A Session with the Doctor: *Answers to Questions Patients Ask Most*

"Man's happiness in life is the result of man's own effort."

CH'EN TU-HSIU, 1879–1942

Q: Does depression have to be present for fusion to occur?

A: No. Depression makes fusion more likely, because depressed people more commonly express the negative emotions of which fusion is made, but even relatively normal people can become fused under certain circumstances. The following fracas that I recently witnessed at a self-serve gas station here in California serves as a good example.

A woman was pumping her gas as a man pulled up to use the set of pumps behind her. He had to pull his car quite close to the woman's in order for the hose to reach his tank, leaving the woman enough—though not a lot of room—to complete the task. She responded to the close quarters he had left her with a sarcastic remark.

216

"Chill out, bitch," was his heated reply.

I won't repeat her retort, but trust that it upstaged his in its profanity. Worse yet, it proceeded to ignite one of the more vituperative verbal exchanges I've witnessed in public for quite some time. A full-blown fusion eruption was in progress between two total strangers, neither of whom was likely to have been clinically depressed, yet both of whom clearly were out of control.

What I found especially interesting, though, was my own reaction to the fight. I felt like leaping in headfirst myself, and had I not had the advantage of a clinical understanding of the situation, I might have. My feelings showed me just how powerful the contagious aspects of fusion can be. I was so annoyed at being subjected to such a high level of negative emotional arousal that I was tempted to make the situation even worse by adding yet more negative arousal of my own. This is how fusion rages out of control in family settings. One person ignites a spark, someone else becomes inflamed, and soon everyone within earshot becomes agitated to the point of being tempted to add to the heat.

So yes, fusion can occur even though depression is not present. It's a universal phenomenon that can occur any time negative emotional arousal between two people surpasses a certain "kindling point" and feelings begin to get out of control. In the situation I've just described, the initial fusion spark was produced by the woman's high level of negative emotional arousal. This produced a fusion eruption when the man felt unfairly attacked and responded with his own high levels of negative emotional arousal.

Q: **Aren't you doing a disservice when you tell someone that his depression is a medical disorder? Doesn't that give the person an excuse to do nothing about it?**

A: A young woman recently asked me that, after I had seen her husband and informed him that his depression was a diag-

nosable medical disorder that could be treated with psychotherapy and appropriate psychiatric medication. She was
furious at me. "Now he thinks he doesn't have to take responsibility for his actions," she said. "He thinks he can just sit back
and let you—and the medications you're giving him—do all the
work."

If you can identify with this woman's concern, all I can tell
you is that you must have patience and faith. The worst thing
you can do is react angrily to the way your loved one responds
to treatment, even if his response does seem to be one of
relinquishing responsibility for his actions. He has made an
important first step in agreeing to receive treatment, and you'll
only be impeding his progress by accusing him of being dis-
honest in his attempt to get help. The woman's husband was
using my diagnosis as a way of continuing to generate conflict
between them, which showed me that he was attempting to
stay fused with her. She, on the other hand, was giving him
what he wanted by allowing his behavior to upset her. She
needed to understand that his reliance on his "disorder" was in
fact a symptom of his disorder; that he didn't yet have the
strength to break free of his depressed role; and that it wasn't
her job to rush him. The pacing of his recovery was up to me.

Keep in mind, too, that you should be thankful if your loved
one's problem is a treatable disorder rather than a less treatable
character flaw. Once treatment is successful, you should see a
substantial change.

Q: My wife recently recovered from a depression, but now I
feel depressed. Could I have caught my depression from
my wife?

A: In a manner of speaking, yes. You may have caught a type
of secondary emotional infection that is quite common with
depression. If you were used to playing a certain role when
your wife was depressed, that role may no longer fit now that
she's well. Her recovery may have forced you into playing a
new role, a role with which you may not feel totally comfort-

able. Maybe you were the strong one when your wife was depressed, but you're feeling like the weak one now that she's well. This happens quite often in relationships when recovery from a depression occurs. People find themselves switching roles in order to keep the old equilibrium of the relationship intact. It sounds to me as though you're becoming the weak one now that your wife is showing the strength.

Don't let it happen. You're going to have to restructure your interactions so that both of you can be strong at the same time. It might not be easy at first, as new boundaries and styles of communicating will need to be established, but it's the only way you're going to be able to achieve a mutually beneficial relationship capable of allowing each of you to grow as you should.

Q: **My son is a manic depressive who is not able to function independently. He'd be living in a park somewhere if everyone in the family were to defuse from him as you recommend. What's your advice for situations like this? Do we just abandon him?**

A: Of course you don't abandon him. But you do defuse from him, and there's an important difference. When you defuse, you disengage—but you still keep watch, and care, and learn things about yourself in the process. No two people have the same capabilities when it comes to dealing with a severely disturbed person, and this is something you must accept. If getting involved with your severely disturbed son would risk making *you* emotionally disturbed, then you'd be doing both of you a disservice. Your first responsibility must be keeping yourself well.

Part of dealing with a severely disturbed person is acknowledging that you have very little power in changing the behavior you find so upsetting. You may even contribute to the upsetting behavior by trying to make such changes. What this means, unfortunately, is that you may simply have to wait until your loved one gets so out of control that the legal system allows for intervention. This waiting period can be highly traumatic for all concerned, but the trauma can be minimized via my defusion strategies. Remain calm, remain rational, and try to keep a safe emotional distance. This won't mean you're abandoning your son, but rather simply doing the best you can to maintain peace amidst the highly charged situation at hand. What you must avoid above all is feeding your son's arousal with arousal of your own. In keeping with the contagious-emotions phenomenon, this could create fusion capable of leading to violence and serious physical harm.

Q: I understand your program and it's working for me, but I'm afraid that if I take it to its conclusion and really start feeling good about myself, I won't want to be with my depressed husband anymore. Can't the process of defusion backfire in this sense by increasing the chance that I'll grow apart from my husband and want to be divorced?

A: Yes, but it's the chance you have to take. You owe it to yourself to be the best you can be, and if that means ending your marriage because your husband is not capable of accepting a healthier you, then the divorce was meant to be. I should remind you, however, that by defusing, you will be increasing, not decreasing, the likelihood that your husband will join you in getting well. Don't think that your self-improvement efforts will in any way be at his expense. On the contrary, they will be to his benefit.

So go ahead and defuse, and do so with the confidence that it's the best thing for you as well as for your husband and your relationship. Yes, it's possible that your husband will not respond well to your improved level of emotional functioning, but as I said, this is the risk you must take. He may continue to be depressed, refuse professional help, and insist on fusing and provoking conflict. If this is the case, and you decide your relationship must be ended, at least you'll be able to approach the separation knowing you did everything you could to give your marriage its best shot. The only time I ever accuse patients of failing in their marriages is if they refuse to give my defusion strategies a try. Becoming emotionally well and better adjusted is *always* the right thing to do.

Q: **I've been fused with my father for years, but he's not well physically and I'm afraid that by defusing, I'll be sacrificing precious time we can still spend together. It would be such a tragedy if he were to die during the period that I was pulling away from him in hopes of making our relationship better. What do I do?**

A: You seem to be confused about what defusion entails. It does not mean permanently terminating contact, but rather improving contact with your father. I can tell you right now that if you and your father have been fused as you say, your relationship is not a healthy or happy one for either of you. Each of you is feeling hurt, misunderstood, and violated—hardly the kind of feelings that make for meaningful and enjoyable communication.

Yes, it's true that you may need to see and talk to your father less, but if you can use my defusion techniques to help you control the anger you feel when your father provokes you, you'll be moving your relationship forward, not backward. Your relationship will not have the intensity that it currently has, but from what you're telling me, the intensity has tired you out. You need to find and then maintain the right emotional distance from your father, a distance from which you can show him you care about him, but also a distance that keeps you from being angered and hurt by him. This will mean knowing what issues between you serve as fusion triggers and making sure they don't get pulled. And it will mean putting limits on the degree to which you allow your father to aggravate you. If you can do these things, you'll find that your relationship with your father will improve, not diminish, and your remaining years with him will be far happier than they would if you were to remain fused.

Q: **What about sex? If I'm trying to defuse from my husband, won't having sex give him the impression that I'm not capable of the kind of emotional independence that defusion requires?**

A: Not necessarily. It's true that the intimacy of sexual activity can create unhealthy feelings of dependency in some people—in women, especially, as many women tend to be more emotional about sex than men—but this is not true for all people. Some of my patients report that sex actually helps to give them strength in their journey to greater independence, as it gives them pleasure as well as helps to maintain their self-esteem. Sex also can help you show that you still care about your loved one during the defusion process—an important component for developing emotional safety and trust.

Some people do find that sexual relations impede their progress toward greater emotional independence, however, so for these people I do feel abstinence is advised. If this is the course you choose to take, be sure to explain *why* you're being abstinent. You don't want your loved one to feel you're withholding sex as a punishment, because this will only defeat your peacemaking efforts. You might also consider nonerotic physical contact such as hand-holding and hugging to communicate affection. The important thing is for your loved one to know that you're with him rather than against him in your defusion efforts. You're not defusing to hurt or abandon him.

Q: **I don't think my husband is depressed; he's just an unfaithful liar and a cheat. If anyone's depressed, it's me, from having to live with him. Can your defusion strategies help someone like me?**

A: Yes. It sounds to me that your husband has some fairly severe emotional problems, even though he may not be clinically depressed, and these problems should be dealt with in the same calm and rational ways that I would suggest you employ if he were depressed. The conflicts between you and your husband are no doubt generating fusion, which is hurting everyone in your family, so you *all* will need to defuse if the turmoil in your household is to be ended. Not only will this help your husband with his emotional troubles, it will help you with your depression.

If you find you're having difficulty defusing, however, don't hesitate to seek professional help. If you are in fact depressed, you may need medication and/or psychotherapy to help give you the support and clarity of mind that defusion will require. It would be helpful, too, if your husband would agree to seek professional help, because even though you may be depressed, it sounds to me that the fusion in your relationship has harmed him perhaps even more than you. If he refuses to go for individual help, conjoint therapy would be a good place to start, with you leading the way to the therapist's office.

Q: **I've learned over the years that it's best just to keep my relationship with my wife as superficial as possible. If I try to talk about anything in depth with her, we inevitably begin to argue. Lately, though, she's been accusing me of being cold and uncaring for not talking with her more. How do I deal with this when I can't win either way?**

A: It sounds to me that your relationship has had problems that existed for many years prior to what you're currently experiencing, but let's deal with the dilemma you presently face. You may be saying things to your own wife that are communicating hostilities or are creating insecurities in her that you are not aware of. She then responds as if she's being attacked, and you respond by feeling falsely accused for having made the attack. This is fusion at its worst, as both of you feel the other is to blame.

What can be done about it?

On the surface, it might seem that you're doing the right thing by reducing your communication with your wife overall, but you must realize that you're doing this to protect yourself as much as your wife. You're avoiding her reactions, which you find so upsetting, and in so doing you're giving her the message that your withdrawal is in fact *her fault*. Your silence is merely confirming to your wife that you feel she's the one responsible for the communication difficulties in your relationship. It's a catch-22 for sure, which you may need professional assistance to escape.

Your wife probably is suffering from significant self-esteem problems. You probably are out of touch not only with your own real feelings about your wife, but how those feelings are subconsciously being communicated in the subtleties of your words, the tone of your voice, and your actions. Your goals for the future of your relationship should be learning to be open with your wife about the fears you have of communicating with her, and being willing to share responsibility for feeling those fears. You're going to have to learn to communicate on a level that you've been unable to do ever since your relationship began.

Q: Is it really so bad just to live with fusion? My wife and I have had a stormy relationship for years, but we love each other. We're just feisty, outspoken people.

A: Many couples tell me this. They have turbulent relationships filled with pain, passion, anger, and love, yet they find the overall result satisfying, and so have no real desire to change. They rather enjoy their emotional roller-coaster ride, in fact, saying that it keeps their marriages feeling "alive."

But alive, unfortunately, does not always mean well. If you have children, first of all, I can assure you that the "excitement" in your marriage is not good for them. All the ups and downs are creating anxieties in your children that could adversely effect both their immediate as well as long-term emotional health.

Then, too, I suspect that your professed enjoyment of the "spice" in your marriage could mean you're less in control than you may think. You could simply be falling into the mold carved out for you by your parents. If their marriage was tumultuous, you could be following in their footsteps, whether they're the best steps for you or not.

So I suggest you at least give peace a chance—if not for yourself, for your children. Even a relatively calm relationship can have emotional highs, physical passion, and stimulating conversations. You don't need the chaos to have your "cake."

Q: I know fusion is bad for one's mental health, but could it also be bad for physical health?

A: Unquestionably. Research has linked the chronic anger and hostility characteristic of fusion with heart disease, ulcers, irritable bowel syndrome, headaches, backache, and even cancer. The connection is thought to be chronic stress. Any overload of mental stress can adversely affect the body physically, and fusion certainly qualifies as a mental-stress overload. The body is kept in a near constant state of arousal by fusion, the result being the release of stress-related body chemicals thought to be a primary factor in the above-mentioned maladies.

As evidence of fusion's harmful effects on the body, I have had more than a few patients report feeling much better physically when they begin to defuse. I've seen backaches get better, headaches resolve, chronic fatigue disappear, and even angina (chest pain caused by coronary artery disease) improve. It all points to just how intimate the connection between the mind and body really is.

Q: I can defuse sometimes, but there are other times when I just can't resist getting caught up in what my boyfriend is

saying or doing, and I get angry and fuse. Am I erasing all the progress we've made up to this point when this happens?

A: No. Relapses are natural and to be expected, and it's important that you know this so you don't overreact and make your relapses worse. Like the dieter who must learn not to go on an eating "binge" because of one small slip, you must learn not to go on an anger binge because of one small slip when defusing. By learning to stop these slips short of full-blown fusion eruptions, you will actually be increasing your feelings of confidence and safety about your relationship, because you'll know that you both have the tools to handle a difficult situation without catastrophic results. Episodes of anger, disappointment, and sadness are inevitable even in the healthiest of relationships, so feel assured that you're in good company if and when your relapses occur.

This is not to say you may let your guard down, however. And should you have a recurrence of a full-scale fusion eruption, you and your loved one must sit down and analyze why. What you must not do is allow the eruption to make you feel hopeless, or to allow it to push your relationship back to where you are both on the brink of the fusion "kindling point" on a day-to-day basis. Remember: Complete protection from emotional upsets is not a realistic goal to have. Don't prevent yourselves from being "good" by trying to be perfect.

Q: **I have two daughters, ages 15 and 11, who fight like cats and dogs. Could they be fused, and could their quarrels in any way be related to the troubles my husband and I are having?**

A: Absolutely. Fusion is not for adults only, and it's especially likely to be a problem when children are living with parents who are fused. Some children will react to fusion between their parents by withdrawing and becoming inwardly fearful and angry, while others will react by being outwardly angry and difficult to control. Either way, the contagious emotions phenomenon is at work as the children "catch" the negative emotional arousal they see and feel being displayed by their parents. This is especially unfortunate because not only does it make children more likely to quarrel among themselves, it makes them more likely to quarrel with their parents, thus adding more negative emotional arousal to the family system as a whole. The greater the number of people participating in this fused system, moreover, the more intense the negative emotional arousal will be. This is why it's so important to control fusion at its original, parental source. The more people fusion reaches, the more momentum it gains and the more damaging it becomes.

Q: How can depression make someone so violent and angry?

A: Depression can distort a person's perception of his environment so much that he may believe he is being slighted, demeaned, rejected, or even attacked. Depending on the person's character structure and basic level of self-esteem, these faulty perceptions can reawaken memories of similar affronts experienced during the person's upbringing. Such reawakenings are known as "narcissistic injuries," and they can cause anger that is quite pronounced in people whose self-worth has been damaged by painful childhood experiences.

Another factor that contributes to emotional volatility in depressed people is the ability of depression to lower tolerance to frustration. A depressed person loses much of his ability to cope, with the result being that he may have considerable trouble remaining calm even in relatively nonthreatening situations. Combine this reduced ability to cope with a central nervous system that already is unnaturally sensitive to agitation due to disordered functioning of the brain, and you can see why depressed people can be such live wires.

Then, too, anger and violence are means by which many depressed people choose to defend themselves. They use their anger to protect themselves from the people and the circumstances in their lives they erroneously believe to be the cause of their depression. Consider, too, that many depressed people abuse alcohol and drugs, the result being even more agitation as substance abuse ultimately does far more to reduce coping ability than to enhance it.

Q: I know this sounds crazy, but I think I'm fused with my wife's cat. The thing seems to hate me as much as my wife. Am I imagining it?

A: Probably not. If you and your wife are not getting along, your wife's cat is probably sensing it. I'm not saying the cat is taking sides, but it is being made jumpy by the turmoil, and even more so if you're displaying anger at the cat directly. You may even be using the cat as a kind of scapegoat for your anger at your wife, in which case the cat has every right to feel uneasy around you.

Should you work to defuse from your pet?

Yes, because it will help you defuse from your wife. Many times pets become unwitting contributors to the fusion between people by being just one more thing to fight about. I wouldn't be surprised, for example, if your wife accused you of being harsh and inconsiderate to her cat, just as she feels you're harsh and inconsiderate to her.

Then, too, a pet can be a contributor to fusion by being a bone of contention in its own right. I treated one woman, whose marriage had been suffering for years because of what her husband called her "horse problem." Roughly 15 percent of their relatively modest gross family income was going toward the boarding and care of her three horses. This served as a fusion trigger, regardless of whatever the real issue of contention may have been between them.

So yes, you can become fused with a pet, and that fusion can add to the fusion between you and your loved one. Perhaps the most extreme example I've observed of this occurred when two patients of mine waged a bitter divorce struggle over who would get the dog. Neither of them really liked the dog, but it gave them a reason to remain fused with each other right to the end.

Q: **Is it always possible to know who's actually the depressed person in a fused relationship? I think it's my wife, and she thinks it's me.**

A: No, it's not always possible to know—but then it's not always necessary, either. Searching for the original source of depression in a fused relationship can be as futile as searching for the beginning of a circle. What's important is knowing that it *is*, in fact, a circle that fusion has created, a closed loop whereby hurtful behavior from one person ignites hurtful behavior from another in a way that winds up hurting each person equally. There are many cases that I have treated very successfully where I am still unsure which partner originally had the depression that started the fusion process. This used to bother me, but in time I learned that it wasn't important to know who started the fusion cycle. What was important was identifying fusion triggers, and then finding ways to break into the fusion cycle so that its destruction could be stopped.

So stop arguing with your wife about who first had the depression that started your fusion cycle. You are only contributing to the fusion by doing so. It's also my guess that it's a moot point at this stage, because you're probably both distraught. What you need to concern yourselves with is ending the fusion in your relationship, not accrediting it.

Q: **You keep talking about learning to manage intimate relationships in a calm and rational manner. But doesn't that take a lot of the spontaneity, romance, and "spice" out of life?**

A: That question was first posed to me by an accomplished artist, a true romantic by anyone's standards who felt life should be an adventure, "not a guided tour." He went on to accuse my defusion strategies of being dispassionate and mechanical, and of stifling the raw emotions he felt were essential for keeping life interesting. "Can relationships really be approached with such robotic objectivity and still be meaningful and fun?" he wanted to know.

It was a valid concern (which I later heard voiced by others), so I knew my answer needed to be carefully considered.

"I'm afraid many of us use what you call the "spice of life" as a cover-up for what in truth may be a bit rotten," I said. I went on to explain that many people use their emotional ups and downs as a way of avoiding the realization that their relationships may actually have very little substance in between. They keep themselves in constant transit between their highs and lows because they have very little enjoyable middle ground to call "home." They'd rather fight or make up, rather than face the fact that their relationships have very little to offer.

My patient seemed surprised and touched by my response, for it described all too well his predicament. He said his relationship with his depressed wife felt as though it had no real foundation, that there was passion, but very little real friendship or trust. "Can those things really be developed?" he wanted to know.

And with that, we were down to the very heart of what I've been saying in this book. Yes, true intimacy in relationships *can* be developed. But it takes work. We seem to operate under the belief that true intimacy in emotional relationships should come spontaneously, instinctively, and naturally—but too often this just isn't so. It requires the same kind of objectivity and attention to detail that success in our careers requires. Making emotional relationships go well is no different from making anything else go well. It requires knowledge and effort. And if the person with whom you're involved is emotionally disturbed, the knowledge and effort will need to be even greater. Relying on instinct alone to chart you through the troubled waters of dealing with someone who's depressed is an invitation to disaster.

Letting go of your emotional reactivity may not be easy at first, because you may miss the turbulence of living life in the fused lane. All I can say is, hold true to your new course. You must learn to replace the highs and lows of fusion with something far better—the healthier and much more durable pleasures of feeling well adjusted and secure. There is extreme pleasure in the sensation of calm happiness that people addicted to fusion never allow themselves to enjoy, and this is the higher emotional ground attained by the process I've described as "spiraling up." Don't miss the chance for this experience. Once off the roller-coaster ride of fusion, you will be better able to discover emotional rewards that only a secure and stable life can bring, rewards that will include greater self-understanding and self-acceptance—perhaps the healthiest and most desirable pleasures of all.

REFERENCES AND
SUGGESTED READING

Beck, A. T., Rush, A. J., Shaw, B. F., and Emery, G. *Cognitive Therapy of Depression*, New York: Guilford Press, 1979.

Burns, David, *Feeling Good—The New Mood Therapy*, New York: William Morrow, 1980.

DSM-IIIR *Diagnostic and Statistic Manual of Mental Disorders*, American Psychiatric Association, 1987.

Gold, M. *The Good News About Depression*, New York: Villard Books, 1986.

Kanfer, F. and Goldstein, A. (editors), *Helping People Change*, Elmsford, NY: Pergamon Press, 1975.

Klerman, G., Weissman, M., Rounsaville, B., and Chevron, E. *Interpersonal Psychotherapy of Depression*, New York: Basic Books, Inc., 1984.

Seligman, Martin, *Helplessness*, San Francisco, CA: W. H. Freeman and Co., 1975.

Weisinger, Hendrie, *The Critical Edge*, New York: Little, Brown, 1988.

Weisinger, Hendrie, *Dr. Weisinger's Anger Workout*, New York: William Morrow, 1985.